First World War
and Army of Occupation
War Diary
France, Belgium and Germany

17 DIVISION
Divisional Troops
Machine Gun Corps
17 Battalion
24 February 1918 - 28 February 1919

WO95/1995/2

The Naval & Military Press Ltd
www.nmarchive.com
Published in association with The National Archives

Published by

The Naval & Military Press Ltd

Unit 10 Ridgewood Industrial Park,

Uckfield, East Sussex,

TN22 5QE England

Tel: +44 (0) 1825 749494

www.naval-military-press.com

www.nmarchive.com

This diary has been reprinted in facsimile from the original. Any imperfections are inevitably reproduced and the quality may fall short of modern type and cartographic standards.

© Crown Copyright
Images reproduced by permission of The National Archives, London, England, 2015.

Contents

Document type	Place/Title	Date From	Date To
Heading	WO95/1995 (2)		
Heading	17th Division 17th Bn Machine Gun Corps 1918 Feb-Feb 1919		
Heading	War Diary of 17th Battalion M.G.C. from 24-2-18 to 28-2-18		
War Diary	Bertincourt	24/02/1918	28/02/1918
Heading	17th Div. 17th Battalion. Machine Gun Corps. March 1918		
Heading	War Diary of 17th Battalion M.G.C. from 1-3-1918 to 31-3-1918		
War Diary	Bertincourt	01/03/1918	22/03/1918
War Diary	Beaulencourt	23/03/1918	23/03/1918
War Diary	Courcellette	24/03/1918	24/03/1918
War Diary	Meaulte	25/03/1918	25/03/1918
War Diary	Henancourt	26/03/1918	26/03/1918
War Diary	Senlis	26/03/1918	26/03/1918
War Diary	Contay	27/03/1918	31/03/1918
Heading	17th Divisional M.G.C. War Diary 17th Battalion Machine Gun Corps April 1918		
Heading	17th Division. 50th Infantry Brigade		
Heading	War Diary of 17th Battalion M.G.C. from 1-4-1918 to 30-4-1918		
War Diary	Contay	01/04/1918	03/04/1918
War Diary	Flesselles	04/04/1918	06/04/1918
War Diary	Berneuil	07/04/1918	09/04/1918
War Diary	Puchevillers	11/04/1918	15/04/1918
War Diary	Varennes	16/04/1918	30/04/1918
Heading	War Diary 17th Battalion M.G.C. from 1-5-1918 To 31-5-1918		
War Diary	Varennes	01/05/1918	08/05/1918
War Diary	Le. Quesnoye	09/05/1918	25/05/1918
War Diary	Acheux	26/05/1918	31/05/1918
Miscellaneous	17th Battalion, M.G.C.	05/07/1918	05/07/1918
Heading	War Diary of 17th Battalion M.G. Corps From 1.6.1918 to 30.6.1918		
War Diary	Acheux	01/06/1918	22/06/1918
War Diary	Acheux Toutencourt	23/06/1918	24/06/1918
War Diary	Toutencourt	25/06/1918	30/06/1918
Miscellaneous	17th Battalion, M.G.C.	03/08/1918	03/08/1918
Heading	War Diary of 17th Battalion M.G Corps From 1.7.1918 to 31.7.1918		
War Diary	Toutencourt	01/07/1918	09/07/1918
War Diary	Toutencourt Harponville (U.11.d.0.2)	10/07/1918	10/07/1918
War Diary	Harponville	11/07/1918	18/07/1918
War Diary	Harponville Forceville. P.27.b.1.2.	19/07/1918	19/07/1918
War Diary	Forceville	19/07/1918	31/07/1918
Heading	17th Divl. Troops 17th Battalion Machine Gun Corps. August 1918		
Heading	War Diary of 17th Battalion M.G.C. From 1.8.18 to 31.8.18 Vol 7		

War Diary	Forceville P.27.b.1.2. Sheet 57d, 1/40,000 & Sheet 57d. S.E. 1/20,000	01/08/1918	01/08/1918
War Diary	Forceville, P.27.b.1.2	02/08/1918	05/08/1918
War Diary	Forceville, P.27.b.1.2. & Herissart. T.5.a.	06/08/1918	06/08/1918
War Diary	Herissart. T.5.a.	07/08/1918	07/08/1918
War Diary	Herissart T.5.a. Bussy Sheet 62d, 1/40,000.	08/08/1918	08/08/1918
War Diary	Bussy. Heilly	09/08/1918	09/08/1918
War Diary	Heilly.	10/08/1918	10/08/1918
War Diary	Heilly Morcourt Q.16.a.4.4. Sheet 62d. 1/40,000 & 62. D. SE. 1/20,000.	11/08/1918	11/08/1918
War Diary	Morcourt. Q.16.a.4.4.	12/08/1918	15/08/1918
War Diary	Morcourt. Q.16.a.4.4. Vecquemont.	16/08/1918	16/08/1918
War Diary	Vecquemont	17/08/1918	17/08/1918
War Diary	Herissart. Smith St Camp. Corps M.G. School. T.5.a.	18/08/1918	18/08/1918
War Diary	Herissart. Corps M.G. 4 School. T.5.a.	19/08/1918	24/08/1918
War Diary	Beaussart. Billet 23. Q.17.c.7.3. Sheet 57D. SE	25/08/1918	25/08/1918
War Diary	Q.17.c.7.3. Sheet 57D. SE.	26/08/1918	26/08/1918
War Diary	Q.17.c.7.3. Gravel Pit At R.34.a.0.4. Sheet 57D. SE.	27/08/1918	27/08/1918
War Diary	Gravel Pit R.34.A.O.4. Sheet 57D. SE.	27/08/1918	29/08/1918
War Diary	Sheet 57D. SE. R. 34. A.O.4. M.28.d.3.O. Sheet 57C. SW.	30/08/1918	30/08/1918
War Diary	M.28.d.3.0. Sheet 57C. SW.	31/08/1918	31/08/1918
Operation(al) Order(s)	17th Battalion, Machine Gun Corps, Order No. 28	20/08/1918	20/08/1918
Heading	War Diary Of 17th Battalion M.G. Corps From 1.9.18 to 30.9.18		
War Diary	Sheet 57C M.28.d.3.O.	01/09/1918	01/09/1918
War Diary	Martinpuich M.28.d.3.O.	02/09/1918	02/09/1918
War Diary	Martinpuich M.28.d.3.O. N. 23.a.2.1.	03/09/1918	03/09/1918
War Diary	Beaulencourt N.23.a.3.0	04/09/1918	05/09/1918
War Diary	Beaulencourt N.23.a.3.0 Lechelle Wood O.36.d.5.9	06/09/1918	06/09/1918
War Diary	Lechelle Wood. O.36.d.5.9.	07/09/1918	10/09/1918
War Diary	Lechelle Wood. O.36.d.5.9. Rocquigny. O.22.d.	11/09/1918	11/09/1918
War Diary	Rocquigny. O.22.d.	12/09/1918	17/09/1918
War Diary	Le Mesnil En Arrouaise. U.11.d.9.1.	18/09/1918	20/09/1918
War Diary	Etricourt. V.3.b.8.8.	21/09/1918	24/09/1918
War Diary	Le Mesnil En Arrouaise. U.5.a.1.4.	25/09/1918	30/09/1918
Heading	War Diary Of 17th Battalion M.G. Corps From 1.10.1918 To 31.10.1918		
War Diary	Sheet 57b 1/40,000. & 57B. NE. 1/20,000. Mesnil-En-Arrouaise. U.5.a.1.4.	01/10/1918	03/10/1918
War Diary	Mesnil-En-Arrouaise. U.5.a.1.4.	04/10/1918	05/10/1918
War Diary	Heudecourt. W.14.d.5.6.	06/10/1918	07/10/1918
War Diary	Heudecourt. W.14.d.5.6. R.32.a.5.8.	08/10/1918	08/10/1918
War Diary	R.32.a.5.8. Vaucelles Wood. M.28.c. & N.16.a.9.5.	09/10/1918	09/10/1918
War Diary	N.16.a.9.5. Clary. O.17.b.2.7. Ford Bn. HQ. Inchy. J.22.d.8.8.	10/10/1918	10/10/1918
War Diary	Clary. O.17.b.2.7 Ford B.H.Q. Inchy. J.22.d.8.8.	10/10/1918	11/10/1918
War Diary	Clary. O.17.b.2.7 Ford Tronquoy. P.1.a.O.7.	12/10/1918	12/10/1918
War Diary	Tronquoy. P.1.a.O.7.	12/10/1918	12/10/1918
War Diary	P.1.a.0.7.	13/10/1918	13/10/1918
War Diary	Forward. Inchy J.22.d.8.8. Rear. Tronquoy P.1.a.O.7.	14/10/1918	18/10/1918
War Diary	Forward. Inchy. J.22.d.8.8. Rear. Tronquoy. P.1.a.O.7.	19/10/1918	22/10/1918
War Diary	Inchy. J. 20.d.8.8.	23/10/1918	25/10/1918
War Diary	Inchy. J.22.d.8.8. Vendigies (Ford) Rear. Ovillers E.23.b.8.1.	26/10/1918	26/10/1918
War Diary	Forward Vendigies. Rear. Ovillers E.23.b.8.1.	27/10/1918	28/10/1918

War Diary	Forward Vendigies. Rear Ovillers. E. 23.b.8.1. Inchy.	29/10/1918	29/10/1918
War Diary	Inchy.	30/10/1918	31/10/1918
War Diary	Sheet 57B.1/40,000. Inchy.	01/11/1918	01/11/1918
War Diary	Inchy. Ford. Vendigies. Rear. Ovillers E.23.b.8.1.	02/11/1918	04/11/1918
War Diary	Ford. Poix-Du-Nord, Rear. Ovillers E.23.b.8.1. Rear. Poix-Du-Nord.	05/11/1918	05/11/1918
War Diary	Poix-Du-Nord La Tete Noire.	06/11/1918	06/11/1918
War Diary	La-Tete-Noire Berlaimont. U.20.d.8.6.	07/11/1918	07/11/1918
War Diary	Berlaimont U.20.d.8.6. Aulnoye.	08/11/1918	08/11/1918
War Diary	Aulnoye.	09/11/1918	11/11/1918
War Diary	Aulnoye. Engle Fontaine.	12/11/1918	12/11/1918
War Diary	Englefontaine Bertry.	13/11/1918	13/11/1918
War Diary	Bertry.	14/11/1918	07/12/1918
War Diary	Masnieres.	08/12/1918	08/12/1918
War Diary	Hermies	09/12/1918	09/12/1918
War Diary	Beugnatre	10/12/1918	10/12/1918
War Diary	Albert	11/12/1918	11/12/1918
War Diary	Lahoussoye	12/12/1918	12/12/1918
War Diary	Breilly-Sur-Somme.	13/12/1918	13/12/1918
War Diary	Le Quesnoy-Sur-Airaines	14/12/1918	31/01/1919
Heading	17th Battalion Machine Gun Corps February 1919 Strength of Battalion at 1-2-19 offices 36 Vol 13		
War Diary	Le Quesnoy Sur Airaines	01/02/1919	28/02/1919

No 95/1995 (2)

17TH DIVISION

17TH BN. MACHINE GUN CORPS

1918 FEB
~~JLY 1917~~ – FEB 1919

Army Form C. 2118.

WAR DIARY
or
INTELLIGENCE SUMMARY.
(Erase heading not required.)

Vol I

Confidential

WAR DIARY
of
17th Battalion. M.G.C.

From 24-2-18 to 28-2-18

Army Form C. 2118.

WAR DIARY
or
INTELLIGENCE SUMMARY.
(Erase heading not required.)

Place	Date	Hour	Summary of Events and Information	Remarks and references to Appendices
BERTINCOURT	24.2.18		The 17th Batt. M.G.C. was formed out of the 4 M.G. Coys in the 19th Division namely:- 50th, 51st, 52nd & 236 Div. Coys. The following officers:-	DB6
			Major D.R. Cadew C.O.	
			Capt. R.G. Kinsey 2nd in command	
			Lieut. A. McIntosh Adjutant	
			" H.J. Dawe T.O.	
			" J.J. Bill 2/i/c 23rd inst.	DB6
			Arrived & took over their duties on the afternoon 23rd inst. The newly room material was borrowed from the 52nd M.G.C. which was at rest & the 19th Div H.Q.	DB6
			The transport of 3 Coys moved in from their Bdys areas	DB6
	24.2.18		236 Coys transport remaining at VELU.	DB6
			Harassing M.G. fire during the night on enemy tracks & rear trenches	

Army Form C. 2118.

WAR DIARY
or
INTELLIGENCE SUMMARY.
(Erase heading not required.)

17th Batt. M.G.C.

Place	Date	Hour	Summary of Events and Information	Remarks and references to Appendices
MARTINCOURT	25-2-18		During the morning & afternoon enemy guns engaged for two of the enemy with good effect. 600 rounds fired. 7500 rounds fired on enemy tracks & trenches during the night. The 52nd Coy relieved the 51st Coy in the line on the left rear front on the night 25th-26th.	DR6
"	26-2-18		Right Brigade. 650 rounds were fired at E.A. during the day. 4000 rounds fired at roads & trench junctions. Left Brigade. 9500 rounds on roads & trenches. Sniping guns engaged many parties.	DR6
"	27-2-18		8800 rounds were fired on targets & roads R. bgade area. 9000 " " " " " " " L. Bde. area. 600 rounds fired at E.A.	DR6
"	28-2-18		R.Bde. 8800 rounds fired on trenches & tracks - Sniping M.G. engaged on movement sunken road. L. Bde. 9500 rounds on track trenches & roads. Sniping M.G. successfully engaged movement at various points.	DR6

David R. Callan Major
Comdg 17 Bn M.G.C.

17th Div.

17th BATTALION, MACHINE GUN CORPS.

M A R C H

1 9 1 8

WAR DIARY
or
INTELLIGENCE SUMMARY.

Army Form C. 2118.

Secret

CONFIDENTIAL

WAR DIARY.
of
17TH BATTALION M.G.C.
from 1=3=1918. to 31=3=1918.

March 1918   Secret   VOL 2

WAR DIARY
INTELLIGENCE SUMMARY
17th BATTN. M.G.C.

Army Form C. 2118.

Place	Date	Hour	Summary of Events and Information	Remarks and references to Appendices
BERTINCOURT	1.3.18.		Strength of Battalion :- Officers 43 Other ranks 773. From this date the M.G. Coys in the Division lose their numbers and are known as follows :— 50th M.G. Coy becomes "A" Coy 52nd M.G. Coy becomes "C" Coy 51st M.G. Coy becomes "B" Coy 236th M.G. Coy becomes "D" Coy 14,400 rounds were fired at the enemy on the Div. Front. Sniping M.Gs engaged enemy parties.	
	2.3.18.		A draft of 9 O.R.s was received from Bde. Bde. transferred in connection with the formation of the BN. 26.ORs received from Inf. Bde. 14,400 rounds fired on enemy roads, tracks &c. 700 rds on E.A. M.Gs.	
	3.3.18.		Capt. Temp. Major D. B. CALDER Royal Highlanders promoted to rank of temp. Lieutenant Colonel. Authority dated 24.2.18. Lt. Col. C. P. P. WINSER. D.S.O. and M.i/D Cox M.C. of 19th Bn. M.G.C. visited BN. H.Q. Lieut. D. IRVIN of "A" Coy. proceeded to ENGLAND 20th Ulst. is struck off the strength. "B" Coy. relieved "A" Coy in the line. 18,000 rounds fired on enemy roads etc. Sniping M.G. active.	
	4.3.18.		Coy Commanders of 19th Bn. M.G.C. visited the Coy. H.Qs in the line preparatory to relieving the manned harassing line on roads, tracks &c. was carried out 18,000 rounds being fired.	

Marshall Lieut. Colonel
Commanding 17 Battn. M.G. Corps

Secret

Army Form C. 2118.

WAR DIARY

or

INTELLIGENCE SUMMARY

(Erase heading not required.)

17TH BATTN. M.G.C.

Instructions regarding War Diaries and Intelligence Summaries are contained in F. S. Regs, Part II. and the Staff Manual respectively. Title pages will be prepared in manuscript.

Place	Date	Hour	Summary of Events and Information	Remarks and references to Appendices
BERTINCOURT.	5.3.18		16,000 rounds fired on enemy trenches, roads &c. 2/Lt. J.W. JONES and 2/Lt. W.R.D. LOOMIS joined from the BASE DEPOT. 2/Lt. by the relief of the BN. by the 19th BN. M.G.C. has been postponed owing to the expectation of a great enemy offensive.	
	6.3.18		20,000 rounds fired on enemy targets. Sniping M.G. hit four of an enemy working party.	
	7.3.18		17,000 rounds fired on selected areas. Sniping guns caused casualties to the enemy. 2/Lt. H.G.P. McILROY appointed 2nd in command of "D" Coy.	
	8.3.18		8,000 rounds fired at trenches and tracks. "C" Coy. relieved by "A" Coy. in the left sector. 2/Lt. F. HYDE appointed 2nd in command of "C" Coy. 2/Lt. A.R. FRASER " " " " " " "B" Coy.	
	9.3.18		Eight M.Gs. were placed into position in the HERMIES 20,000 rounds fired on the usual targets DEFENCES. Parties of the enemy were dispersed by the sniping guns during the day and several casualties were inflicted. Two of the "A.A" M.Gs. fired at the leading machine of an enemy squadron at 11.30 a.m. Strong tracer bullets were observed to hit the plane which thereupon turned back towards the enemy lines. 2/Lt. W.C. SANDERS and 10. O.R. joined from the Base.	

David A Ballet
LIEUT. COLONEL,
COMMANDING 17 BATTN. M.G. CORPS.

Secret

Army Form C. 2118.

WAR DIARY
or
INTELLIGENCE SUMMARY.
(Erase heading not required.)

17th BATTN. M.G.C.

Instructions regarding War Diaries and Intelligence Summaries are contained in F.S. Regs., Part II. and the Staff Manual respectively. Title pages will be prepared in manuscript.

Place	Date	Hour	Summary of Events and Information	Remarks and references to Appendices
BERTINCOURT	10.3.18.		16,500 rounds fired at various roads &c. 181. O.R. received from Inf. Bdes. to be transferred to M.G. Bn. in connection with the new formation.	
	11.3.18.		Four guns permanently placed in position at Fort Robertson. 19,000 rounds expended at various targets. Sniping guns engaged targets with good result. 1.O.R. joined the Bn. from the 10th Sherwood Foresters. Bn. Sports Committee formed under the presidency of Capt. T.G. Kinsey M.C.	
	12.3.18.		21,000 rounds searched and raked many few targets for sniping guns.	
	13.3.18.		20,500 rounds fired on special targets. "A.A." M.Gs. fired on many E.A. and destroyed in two cases forced formations to scatter. "D" Coy had a gun destroyed by shell-fire.	
	14.3.18.		19,000 rounds engaged centres of enemy movement. 2Lt. J.A. Wilby and 6.O.R. joined the Bn. from the Base.	
	15.3.18.		22,750 rounds fired on well used tracks. Sniping guns fired on enemy working parties.	

David Baedes,
LIEUT. COLONEL,
COMMANDING 17 BATTN. M.G.C.

Secret

Army Form C.2118.

WAR DIARY
or
INTELLIGENCE SUMMARY. 17TH BATTN. M.G.C.
(Erase heading not required.)

Instructions regarding War Diaries and Intelligence Summaries are contained in F. S. Regs., Part II. and the Staff Manual respectively. Title pages will be prepared in manuscript.

Place	Date	Hour	Summary of Events and Information	Remarks and references to Appendices
BERTINCOURT	16.3.18		18,700 rounds fired on enemy work by 1.O.P. of "A" Coy.	
	17.3.18		23,350 rounds expended by M.G. fire against dumps, trenches, E.A. & enemy snipping guns. One man with own to be carried away on stretcher. 2.O.P.'s of "A" Coy were accidentally gassed by our own gas projectors. A man M.G. was severed to replace the one "D" Coy had destroyed.	
	18.3.18		13,150 rounds expended on reveal points of enemy activity observed by "C" Coy.	
	19.3.18		21,050 rounds fired on enemy trenches. Lt. Col. C.R.P. WINSER D.S.O. and officers of the 19th Bn. M.G.C. visited BN.HQ. and the line to relieve.	
	20.3.18		18,000 rounds were expended in searching and traversing various roads and areas. Parties of the enemy were dispersed by the snipping guns. 4 guns of "B" Coy interchanged positions with 4 guns of "D" Coy in the HERMIES DEFENCES. 1.O.P.'s of "C" Coy were wounded by a shell. Orders to relief by the 19th Bn. M.G.C. issued to all concerned.	

David Blaser
LIEUT. COLONEL,
COMMANDING 17 BATTN. M.G. CORPS.

Secret

Army Form C. 2118.

Instructions regarding War Diaries and Intelligence Summaries are contained in F.S. Regs., Part II. and the Staff Manual respectively. Title pages will be prepared in manuscript.

WAR DIARY
or
INTELLIGENCE SUMMARY. 17th BATTN. M.G.C.
(Erase heading not required.)

Place	Date	Hour	Summary of Events and Information	Remarks and references to Appendices
BERTINCOURT	21.3.18	10.15 a.m.	The expected enemy offensive has begun. HUGHES TRENCH was attacked at 10.15 a.m. and all S.O.S. M.Gs fired on Barrage lines. The guns in the front system – where the attack was certainly first broke out of enemy concentrations and inflicted many casualties. The four guns held in Div. reserve are now in position at the SPOIL HEAP and placed under the control of the BRIGADE in support. Although the enemy artillery shelled the whole of the Div. front, none of the M.Gs were knocked out. The enemy attack was successfully repulsed and largely responsible for the Div. line maintained. M.Gs of the Div. front, in large numbers M.Gs E.A. patrolled the Div. front, at a good height. All during the day but were were responsible for A.A. M.Gs. A prisoner captured this morning states that artillery was completely frustrated with the attack on HUGHES TRENCH and was forced to move from GRAINCOURT against HAVRINCOURT, which had many yards from by M.G. fire before the enemy had reached his assembly positions S.W. of GRAINCOURT. 2. O.Rs. joined the Bn. from the BASE. "B" Echelon withdrew to BEAULEN COURT.	

David Balder
LIEUT. COLONEL,
COMMANDING 17. BATTN.

Secret

Army Form C.2118.

WAR DIARY
or
INTELLIGENCE SUMMARY
(Erase heading not required.)

17TH BATTN. M.G.C.

Place	Date	Hour	Summary of Events and Information	Remarks and references to Appendices
BERTINCOURT	22/3/18 (a).	1.30 a.m.	Evacuation of the front system of defence ordered to commence. "A" "D" and "C" Coy commanders received orders from the Brigades to which they were attached. O.C. "D" Coy received no information of the warning orders sent out from Bn. H.Q. and failed to reach "D" Coy. The control of all M.G.C. was placed into the hands of G. Oz. C. BRIGADES with the exception of 12 guns which were formed into DIVISIONAL reserve at SPOIL HEAP (J.36). The guns in the HERMIES — FORT ROBERTSON — HAVRINCOURT Quarry became a front system of guns. "A" Coy. In accordance with the 50th Bde orders, took up positions in MAXWELL AVEN. One of these guns and 8 guns of "A" Coy which took action at 2.30 p.m. of the remaining 8 guns of "A" Coy, after evacuating the front system, took up a position at SPOIL HEAP (J.36) & with orders received moved to HERMIES in front on as follows : 6 guns in HERMIES the 51st. Syd Bde. H.Q. HERMIES. (5.45 p.m.) QUARRY. 2 guns at out of action. One of these guns attacked the third line of defence and "B" Coy. O.C. reconnoitred suitable gun positions for use if necessary	

David B Baeder
LIEUT. COLONEL
COMMANDING 17 BATTN. M.G. CORPS.

Army Form C. 2118.

Secret

WAR DIARY
or
INTELLIGENCE SUMMARY. 17TH BATTN. M.G.C.

(Erase heading not required.)

Instructions regarding War Diaries and Intelligence Summaries are contained in F.S. Regs., Part II. and the Staff Manual respectively. Title pages will be prepared in manuscript.

Place	Date	Hour	Summary of Events and Information	Remarks and references to Appendices
BERTINCOURT.	22/3/18 (a)	11 a.m.	All the guns (twelve) in the HERMIES defences in action when the enemy attacked HERMIES in force at 11 a.m. The village was heavily shelled but when the attack took place the M.G. fire continued and did great execution. The enemy approached to within 30 yards of one gun but was effectively dealt with.	
		4.30 p.m.	The enemy attacked HERMIES for the second time after massing on the DOIGNIES and DEMICOURT roads. The attack was also broken up by rifle and M.G. fire. All this time guns were in action at HERMIES (J.36) two of the four guns held a position on the YORKSHIRE SPOIL BANK and two were about to the CHEETHAM SWITCH according to Div. orders. "C" Coy. after evacuating the front system according to orders though then up positions in FORT ROBERTSON - four guns augmented the defences of HAVRINCOURT, and the remaining 8 (eight) passed through the second line into Div. reserve in the LONG VALLEY in front of RUYAULCOURT. Officers were sent forward to reconnoitre the THIRD SYSTEM. Three positions with the infantry being maintained in front of the THIRD SYSTEM. "D" Coy. three guns in GLARGES AVEN. and four guns in the BACKWORTH SPOIL HEAP line were withdrawn in accordance with the general retirement and took up positions	

David R. Ballet
LIEUT. COLONEL.
COMMANDING 17 BATTN. M.G. CORPS.

Army Form C. 2118.

WAR DIARY
or
INTELLIGENCE SUMMARY. 17TH BATTN. M.G.C.
(Erase heading not required.)

Instructions regarding War Diaries and Intelligence Summaries are contained in F.S. Regs., Part II. and the Staff Manual respectively. Title pages will be prepared in manuscript.

Place	Date	Hour	Summary of Events and Information	Remarks and references to Appendices
BERTINCOURT	22/3/18 (C.)		HERMIES – FORT ROBERTSON – HAVRINCOURT defences and materially assisted in repulsing unsuccessful enemy attacks on this line.	
		6/25 am	HAVRINCOURT was attacked at 6.25 pm.	
		7/20 pm	All enemy attacks on the line were beaten off largely by M.G. fire.	
		7/45 pm	and in each case the enemy was beaten off largely by shells.	
			Bn. H.Q. was maintained at BERTINCOURT which was shelled by the enemy at intervals throughout the day. "B" Echelon still at BEAULENCOURT. LT. W.S. TANNER wounded at duty. CAPT. DAVIS rejoined and was sent to "B" Echelon. The front line was ordered along the HERMIES – YORKSHIRE SPOIL BANK – METZ SWITCH defences. During the day the M.G. personnel of the whole DIV. was ordered to this movement. Eight M.Gs. of "C" Coy. through the GREEN LINE which was held by the 47th & 63rd and 2nd DIVS.	
BEAULENCOURT	23.3.18	4am	Empty limbers were sent to suitable points to assist the M.G. Coys. in their withdrawal. Bn. H.Q. closed at BERTINCOURT and re-opened at BEAULENCOURT where they moved to positions at N.11.a.6.5.	

Davy Blacket
LIEUT. COLONEL,
COMMANDING 17 BATTN. M.G. CORPS.

Army Form C. 2118

WAR DIARY
or
INTELLIGENCE SUMMARY 17TH BATTN. M.G.C.
(Erase heading not required.)

Instructions regarding War Diaries and Intelligence Summaries are contained in F. S. Regs., Part II. and the Staff Manual respectively. Title pages will be prepared in manuscript.

Place	Date	Hour	Summary of Events and Information	Remarks and references to Appendices
BEAULEN COURT	23.3.18		became Div. reserve. 2/Lt. R.H. KINGHAM "B" Coy. KILLED — IN — ACTION. 2/Lt. H.S. MILLS "D" Coy. WOUNDED — IN — ACTION. 2/Lt. W.C. SAUNDERS "B" Coy. WOUNDED — IN — ACTION.	
COURCELLETTE	24.3.18		"B" and "D" Coys. moved with the 51st Inf. Bde. to the line at ROCQUIGNY to fill up a gap between ROCQUIGNY and SAILLY SAILLISEL. Each of these companies took 8 guns. "A" Coy joined the 50th Inf. Bde. to assist in protecting the right flank of the Corps front with 12 guns. "C" Coy with 8 guns placed at the disposal of the 52nd Inf. Bde. and marched to ROCQUIGNY.	
		3.40 p.m.	Withdrawal from this line commenced at 3.40 p.m. to GUEDECOURT. FLERS LINE later to the MARTINPUICH – BAZENTIN-LE-GRAND line. "B" Echelon moved to position near the main ALBERT Rd. east of LE SARS & COURCELLETTE and later moved on to HENENCOURT. Bn. H.Q. moved to COURCELLETTE. where all stragglers were collected and returned to the line. Lieut. GOWRING rejoined at COURCELLETTE and was sent in of 8 guns to assist the PIONEER Bn and R.E.s under the command of Col. JAMES to fill up a gap in the line between GOUDECOURT and FLERS. A new Vickers M.G. reserve from D.A.D.O.S.	

Daviobader
LIEUT. COLONEL,
COMMANDING 17 BATTN. M.G. CORPS

Secret

Army Form C. 2118.

WAR DIARY
or
INTELLIGENCE SUMMARY

17TH BATTN. M.G.C.

(Erase heading not required.)

Instructions regarding War Diaries and Intelligence Summaries are contained in F.S. Regs., Part II. and the Staff Manual respectively. Title pages will be prepared in manuscript.

Place	Date	Hour	Summary of Events and Information	Remarks and references to Appendices
MEAULTE	25.3.18		All available M.Gs (36 in number) distributed amongst various Bdes now taken up from shell-fire Bn. "A" Coy report have all left yesterday at dawn on BAZENTIN LE GRAND – MONTAUBAN line to be in action. The teams now acting as infantry and M.G. and M.Gs destroyed in action. Capt Gow ##RING reports that S.M.Gs were in action. The remaining teams of "B" Echellon moved to LAVIEVILLE. Bn. H.Q. moved to MEAULTE. Several casualties caused by enemy aircraft, by M.G. fire when they were flying low. All stragglers reporting at Bn H.Q. went to the Infantry. Retirement still continued to the Bray – ALBERT – ANCRE line from ALBERT to AUCHENVILLERS. Bn. H.Q. moved to HENANCOURT. A.B. & D. Coys rejoined from BDES. Men rested and food given and carried out. "C" Coy still under orders of the 52nd BDE – who are attached to this 9th Div. J. Coy in billets at HENANCOURT and retiring Re-organisation	
HENANCOURT	26.3.18			

David Rhoades
LIEUT. COLONEL
COMMANDING 17 BATTN. M.G. CORPS

ORDERLY ROOM
17 BATTN. M.G. CORPS

Army Form C. 2118.

WAR DIARY
or
INTELLIGENCE SUMMARY. 17th BATTN. M.G.C.
(Erase heading not required.)

Place	Date	Hour	Summary of Events and Information	Remarks and references to Appendices
SENLIS	26.3.18	5 p.m.	Orders received for the advance of the DIVN. to SENLIS to commence at 6 a.m. "C" Coy returned to BN. Coy attached to BDES as follows:— "A" Coy to 50th INF. BDE with 10 M.Gs. "B" Coy to 51st. INF. BDE with 12 M.Gs. "C" Coy to 52nd. INF. BDE with 12 M.Gs. Guns taken up DERNANCOURT – MORLANCOURT – South to the SOMME. Received from D.A.D.O.S. 11 new guns. 400 belts + boxes. 11 Tripods. These guns together with those remaining in the BN. were distributed as above. Owing to the fact that the guns were mounted on tripods and makeshifts were adopted for the Pack animal and machine gun in action found sufficient to meet any emergency left at "B." Echelon.	
CONTAY	27.3.18	1 a.m.	At 1 a.m. BN. H.Q. with "D" Coy with attached there arriving there about 3 a.m. The situation South of ALBERT has been cleared up and the following dispositions carried out. "C" Coy with 52nd BDE at SENLIS. "B" Coy with 51st BDE at MILLENCOURT. "A" Coy with 50th BDE at HENANCOURT. "D" Coy with BN. HQ at CONTAY.	

Burns Baller
LIEUT. COLONEL,
COMMANDING 17 BATTN. M.G. CORPS.

Secret

WAR DIARY
INTELLIGENCE SUMMARY

17th BATTN. M.G.C.

Army Form C. 2118.

Place	Date	Hour	Summary of Events and Information	Remarks and references to Appendices
CONTAY	27.3.18 (contd)		"B" + "C" Coys. with 51st + 52nd Inf. Bdes. relieved the 35th Inf. Bde. and troops of the 63rd Div. in the line. "D" Bn. Echelon still at PUCHEVILLERS. 21 New M.G's received late from the 22nd inst. owing to constant change of SAA was a difficulty, matter of ration, water and dispositions. Rations were distributed at SENLIS. "F" Coy. took up positions in the vicinity of BOUZINCOURT. Seven guns in all being placed into position. Three guns were kept in reserve at SENLIS. "B" Coy. placed 8 guns into positions in front of MILLENCOURT, the last 4 guns in reserve. "C" Coy. still at HENANCOURT. "D" Coy. sent 8 guns to SENLIS where positions were selected in front of SENLIS MILL. Remainder of the Bn. remained at CONTAY.	
	28.3.18		"B" Echelon advanced from PUCHEVILLERS to CONTAY. "A" Coy. have placed four more guns into positions in neighbourhood of BOUZINCOURT, making eleven guns in all. "B" Coy. still maintain 8 guns in positions. "C" Coy. still at HENANCOURT. "D" Coy. + "B" Coy. were relieved	
	29.3.18		at BOUZINCOURT by "C" Coy.	

David B Baker
LIEUT. COLONEL,
COMMANDING 17 BATTN. M.G. CORPS.

Secret

WAR DIARY
or
~~INTELLIGENCE SUMMARY.~~ 17TH BATTN. M.G.C.
(Erase heading not required.)

Army Form C. 2118.

Place	Date	Hour	Summary of Events and Information	Remarks and references to Appendices
CONTAY.	29.3.18 (contd.)		Extract from DIV. letter of appreciation. "The Divi. has had to face situations of extraordinary difficulty and has, in meeting them, earned the appreciation of Higher Authorities and the Honour of being mentioned specially in his official despatches by the Commander-in-Chief."	
			Dispositions unchanged.	
	31/3/18	5.30pm	"B" Coy relieved "A" Coy in the Left Sector the enemy attempted a raid on the Right Sector along the ALBERT — MILLENCOURT Rd. About a hundred of the enemy broke through the line but the forward M.G. got into action and quickly dispersed and disorganised this party. No further attacks materialised. Officers admitted to hospital. The following officers— 2d. C.E.I. LEWIS "C" Coy. 2d. C.G. WHEELER "C" Coy. 2d. J.M. LAWTHER "B" Coy.	

David B. Baxter
LIEUT. COLONEL,
COMMANDING 17 BATTN. M.G. CORPS.

WAR DIARY
INTELLIGENCE SUMMARY.
17th Battn. M.G.C.

Place	Date	Hour	Summary of Events and Information	Remarks
CONTAY.	31.3.18		From the 21st of this month to date the casualties to O.R. were as follows:— 12 Killed in action. 72 Wounded in action. 4 Wounded (gas) 9 Wounded at duty. 2 Wounded and missing 50 Missing. Strength of Battalion:— Officers 43. Other ranks 785.	

David Bailey
LIEUT. COLONEL.
COMMANDING 17 BATTN. M.G. CORPS.

17th Divisional M.G.C.

WAR
DIARY

17th BATTALION

MACHINE GUN CORPS

APRIL 1918

17th Division.
50th Infantry Brigade

Army Form C. 2118.

WAR DIARY
or
INTELLIGENCE SUMMARY.
(Erase heading not required.)

SECRET.

CONFIDENTIAL

WAR DIARY
of
17TH BATTALION M.G.C.
From 1-4-1918 to 30-4-1918.

WAR DIARY
or
INTELLIGENCE SUMMARY

Army Form C. 2118.

SECRET
17th BATTN M.G.C.

Place	Date	Hour	Summary of Events and Information	Remarks and references to Appendices
CONTAY	1/4/18		Strength of Battalion 43 Officers 785 Other ranks. "A" Coy at HENENCOURT. "C" Coy at MILLENCOURT. "D" Coy at SENLIS and CONTAY. Lieut Col R. OAKLEY D.S.O. "B" Coy at BOUZINCOURT. Br. H.Q re-entered relieving Lieutenant J.S. WALKER and 2nd Lieut A.S. BOLDING. Joined from Base while reinforcements received from Base. 181 O.R's.	
	2/4/18		"D" Coy 12th Bn. M.G. C. relieved "C" Coy "B" Coy 12th Bn M.G.C. relieved "B" Coy "A" Coy remained in HENENCOURT infantry Brigade. "B" Coy 17th Bn. relieved 8 guns of "A" Coy G.O.C. 50th BOUZINCOURT and SENLIS M.G.C. 12th Bn M.G.'s at On relief M.G. and "C" Coy Millencourt. CONTAY "D" Coy now had all guns in the CORPS LINE, and the necessary transport at SENLIS. Other dispositions unchanged.	
	3/4/18		"A" Coy moved to CONTAY	
FLESSELLES	4/4/18		Battalion M.T. with "A" "B" any "C" Coys marched to FLESSELLES and went into billets transport moved also. "D" Coy still remained at MILLENCOURT - ENGLEBELMER LINE under control of the 12 Bn, Battn, M.G.C. 1 O.R. "D" Coy killed in action. 2 O.R's wounded.	

Geo? Oakley
LIEUT. COLONEL,
COMMANDING 17 BATTN. M.G. CORPS.

WAR DIARY
or
INTELLIGENCE SUMMARY

SECRET
17TH BATTN M.G.C.

Army Form C. 2118.

Place	Date	Hour	Summary of Events and Information	Remarks and references to Appendices
FLESSELLES	5/4/18		"A" "B" and "C" Coy. reorganised company of 12th Bon. M.G.C. at O.R.s. killed 7. O.P.s. wounded 4.	
	6/4/18		"A" "B" and "C" Coy. paraded under "D" Coy. relieved by B Section of a their muster roll for Commander. during the night, and were accommodated "D" and "C" Coy. marched from WARLOY to MONTONVILLERS and were accommodated in billets. 30 O.R.s. received from D.1.D.O.S. Orders were received to move to BERNEUIL and GORGES Battn. marched to the new area and took over FLESSELLES - HAVERNAS - CANAPLES and was accommodated in billets as follows:- B.H.Q. "B" C. and "D" Coy. together with their Transport at BERNEUIL. "A" Coy. and Transport "D" Coy at GORGES.	
BERNEUIL	7/4/18		CAPT. C.G. SCHURR. R.A.M.C. Sr. joined from 51st Field Ambulance. LIEUT. J.S. [illegible] joined from 52nd Staff Battalion. Reorganisation of Battalion. CAPT. R.G. KINSEY M.C. promoted to Acting Major. TEMP. LIEUT. A. McINNES promoted to Acting Captain.	
	8/4/18		LT.COLONEL D.B. CALDER attended Conference at 17th DIV H.Q. and held a conference with Coy. Commanders at Bn. H.Q.	
PUCHEVILLERS	9/4/18		Bn. marched to PUCHEVILLERS. Batts. H.Q. and "D" Coy in billets, others under canvas.	

David [Calder]
LIEUT. COLONEL,
COMMANDING 17 BATTN. M.G. CORPS.

SECRET

WAR DIARY
or
INTELLIGENCE SUMMARY.   17TH BATTN. M.G.C.

Army Form C. 2118.

Place	Date	Hour	Summary of Events and Information	Remarks and references to Appendices
PUCHEVILLERS	7/4/18		Whole Bn. moved to an and E of PUCHEVILLERS into various camps. Received 15 tripods from D.A.D.O.S. q 13 Bn.	
	13/4/18		Lt.Colonel BACALDER visited 63rd (R.N) M.G. Bn. CORPS LINE at ENGLEBELMER. Reconnoitred 2nd Lt. HARRG. KINSEY M.G.C. quit the Coy Commander. O. Bo. & S.P. with 63rd (R.N) Battn. M.G.C. for reference relief.	
	14/4/18		"B" and "D" Coys. Ambid and 2 Coys of 63rd (R.N) M.G.Bn. in the line under centrol of that Bn. relieving a Coy in keft on the Right sector and "D" Coy. one on VARENNES — AUTHIE-RAFAL.	
	15/4/18		2 O.R. from "A" Coy. joined from base camp at VARENNES and at night relieved a Coy of 63rd (R.N) Battn. in the left sub sector. "D" Coy. relieved a Coy in the support line having five guns in reserve at VARENNES.	
VARENNES	16/4/18		"C" Coy. marched from camp at VARENNES and became DIV. RESERVE. Bn. H.Q. and transport moved to VARENNES and H.Q. opened at Billet number 3. (F.26 c.00.30). 10 a.m. 8 O.R. joined Bn from Divisional Signals joined Bn. from British Army M.G. Depôt (Lt Payries) CAPT. W. FRANKLIN. LIEUT. T.H. UNDERWOOD. "D" Coy.] reverted at LIEUT. H.T. DAWE H.Q. 1550 rounds fired against enemy aircrap. M.G. 25 Light Sales reported in action. 1 O.R "A" Coy. wounded.	
	17/4/18			

David R Balder
LIEUT. COLONEL.
COMMANDING 17 BATTN. M.G. CORPS.

Army Form C. 2118.

SECRET

WAR DIARY
or
INTELLIGENCE SUMMARY. 17th BATTN. M.G.C.

(Erase heading not required.)

Place	Date	Hour	Summary of Events and Information	Remarks and references to Appendices
VARENNES	19/4/18		Recreation room opened for H & O's and Men in Billet No 7. Enemy fired 100 at enemy aircraft.	
	20/4/18		2 guns of "B" Coy transferred into Intermediate line. 2 guns of "A" and one of "C" Coy transferred into Intermediate line. 500 rounds fired at E.A.	
	21/4/18		1 O.R. "D" Coy wounded. 2 more guns of "B" Coy transferred to Intermediate line. 500 rounds fired at E.A.	
	22/4/18		During a counter attack at 4.30 am an S.O.S. guns fired on Barrage lines 9,750 rounds. 1 O.R. "B" Coy wounded. Capt. J.S. GOWRIE recommended arrangements of "B" Coy by "C". Right sector and postponed awaiting Capt. "B" Coy wounded in	
	23/4/18		Reliefs of "D" Coy by "C" Coy. Owing to "C" Coy positioned owing to Infantry relief being demanded from village to open country (1 mile S.W.)	
	24/4/18		Relief again postponed.	

LIEUT. COLONEL,
COMMANDING 17 BATTN. M.G. CORPS.

Army Form C. 2118.

WAR DIARY
or
INTELLIGENCE SUMMARY. 17TH BATTN. M.G.C.

SECRET.

(Erase heading not required.)

Instructions regarding War Diaries and Intelligence Summaries are contained in F. S. Regs., Part ORDERLY ROOM and the Staff Manual respectively. Title pages will be prepared in manuscript.

Place	Date	Hour	Summary of Events and Information	Remarks and references to Appendices
VARENNES	25/4/18		M.G. 2 "A" Coy destroyed by shell fire. "B" Coy relieved in the Right sector by "C" Coy. 20 P.S. "A" Coy killed 2 O.R. wounded 1 "A" Coy 1 B[?] A.2. A.2. moved to CAFÉ de JEUNESSE causing the killed No 3. doing damage to shell fire. 3000 rounds fired at targets in THIEPVAL WOOD. "D" Coy relieved "A" Coy in the Left sector. "A" Coy moved into Corps Line 1 O.R. "C" Coy killed in action 4 O.R. (2, A.2. 1 "A" Coy. 1 "D" Coy) wounded in action. "B" Coy moved out of VARENNES. under canvas at O. 30. b. 4. 2.	
	26/4/18		Promotions and Appointments:— Lieut. A. R. FRASER to command "D" Coy. Lieut. J. S. WALKER to assist in command of "B" Coy. Capt. D. H. HAUGH. "B" Coy to be Acting Major. " J. S. GOWRING. "C" Coy " " " " E. W. DAVIS. "A" Coy " " " Lieut. A. R. FRASER "D" Coy " " " Lieut. H. E. SMITH "A" Coy to be Acting Captain. " J. S. WALKER "B" Coy " " " " H. G. McILROY "C" Coy " " " 2/Lieut. F. HYDE " " "	

[signature]
LIEUT. COLONEL,
COMMANDING 17 BATTN. M.G. CORPS.

WAR DIARY or INTELLIGENCE SUMMARY.

SECRET
17th BATTN. M.G.C.

Army Form C. 2118.

(Erase heading not required.)

Instructions regarding War Diaries and Intelligence Summaries are contained in F.S. Regs., Part II and the Staff Manual respectively. Title pages will be prepared in manuscript.

Place	Date	Hour	Summary of Events and Information	Remarks and references to Appendices
VARENNES.	27/4/18		Bn. H.Q. moved of VARENNES. At 2.30 p.m. S.O.S. sent up on the right sector, country under canvas at O.26.b.4.2. 9000 rounds fired on various targets found all S.O.S. lines opened fire and S.O.S. guns opened fire. 1 O.R. "C" Coy wounded at duty. Authority D.R.O. No 705 dated 26.4.1918 delegated by His Majesty the King, the field Marshall commanding in Chief his awarded the following decorations to the undermentioned N.C.Os and men of the battalion.	
			No. 32316 Pte. E. Paul "D" Coy — MILITARY MEDAL
			114098 " W. CALLAGHER "D" Coy — do
			717713 " J. MORAN "C" Coy — do
			66821 Corpl. R. SPIRING "C" Coy — do
			57228 S/C A.J. PENDRILL "A" Coy — do
			3670 " A.J. EUSTON "B" Coy — do
			115145 a/s/c P.W. HOBBS "C" Coy — do
			143310 " H. SANGSTER "C" Coy — do
			63452 " J.R. LLOYD "B" Coy — do
	28/4/18		6250 rounds fired on roads and various junctions.
Lieut. STANLEY HENRY "A" Coy)
2 Lieut. HORACE S. MILLS "D" Coy) Received certificates for gallantry
2 Lieut. ALFRED W. HIGGINS "B" Coy) and devotion to duty from
1 Otter Tanks.) G.O.C. Division.	

DWMBauer
LIEUT. COLONEL,
COMMANDING 17 BATTN. M.G. CORPS.

Army Form C. 2118.

WAR DIARY
or
INTELLIGENCE SUMMARY.

SECRET.
17TH BATTN. M.G.C.

(Erase heading not required.)

Place	Date	Hour	Summary of Events and Information	Remarks and references to Appendices
VARENNES.	29/4/18		3,300 rounds expended on selected targets. 750 rounds fired on E.A. 1 O.R. "C" Coy wounded at duty. Extract from D.R.O.s. No.2522. Sergt No. 2523 and No. 2522 under authority delegated by His Majesty the King, the shield Marshall Commanding in Chief, awarded the following decorations:— LIEUT. HARRY EDWINSON SMITH "A" Coy. MILITARY CROSS. 2/LIEUT. HERBERT A. DISNEY "D" Coy. —"— French Decoration No. 2596 SGT. R.Y. TEMPLE "A" Coy. MEDAILLE MILITAIRE.	
	30/4/18		"A" Coy relieved "C" Coy. in the Right sector, "C" Coy. now in CORPS. LINE. 3,500 rounds fired on Cross-roads and tracks. a new M.G. received from R.A.O.S. 20 O.Rs. joined Bn from 10th Lancashire Fusiliers. 20 O.Rs. —"— "— 12th Manchester Regt. Strength of Battalion:— 39 Officers 836 Other ranks.	

Darnell Butler
LIEUT. COLONEL,
COMMANDING 17 BATTN. M.G. CORPS.

ORDERLY ROOM
17 BATTN. M.G. CORPS

CONFIDENTIAL

WAR DIARY

OF

17TH BATTALION M.G.C.

From 1-5-1918 to 31-5-1918.

WAR DIARY
or
INTELLIGENCE SUMMARY

SECRET

17TH BATTN. M.G.

Army Form C. 2118.

Place	Date	Hour	Summary of Events and Information	Remarks and references to Appendices
VARENNES	1.5.918		Strength of Battalion 39 Officers 836 Other ranks. "B" Coy relieved "D" Coy in the left Sector. "D" Coy now Divisional Reserve at O.36.b.4.2. 1.O.R. "A" Coy, 1 O.R. "C" Coy wounded in Action.	
	2.5.1918		Rearrangement of boys in the line, according to a new Brigade Front, commenced. 5 guns of "A" Coy interchanged with 5 guns of "C" Coy. 2500 rounds fired on crossroads 1.O.R. "A" Coy Killed in Action. Fired at A.O.S. heavily.	
	3.5.1918		Battalion assault found for Divisional Duty and approximate strength of Officers & O.R. on road used by enemy. "B" Coy and "C" Coy interchanged guns according to the Brigade Front seldom newly disposition of Coys. was as follows:— "A" Coy. Right Brigade Sector. "B" Coy. Left Brigade Sector. "C" Coy. Reserve Brigade Sector. 2/Lt. W.T. PEARCE "B" Coy evacuated to England sick. 5.O.R. "B" Coy wounded in action.	

Ravenhill
Lt Colonel
COMMANDING 17 BATTN. M.G. CORPS.

WAR DIARY or INTELLIGENCE SUMMARY

Army Form C. 2118.

SECRET

17th. BATTN. M.G.C.

Place	Date	Hour	Summary of Events and Information	Remarks and references to Appendices
VARENNES	4/5/18		3500 rounds fired on roads. Lieut. Colonel E.R. McCREADY M.C. and Lieutenant M.D.L. RIDLEY visited Battalion Headquarters. Second in Command, 63rd. (R.N.) Battalion in action. 1.O.R. "A" Coy & 1.O.R. "C" Coy remained in action.	
	5/5/18		1800 rounds fired on fronts of enemy activity. Battalion Headquarters moved from ENGLEBELMER, rode open way to rear section Brigade Headquarters, except "C" Coy, which moved to rear section headquarters. Lieut. Colonel D.B. CALDER visited 63rd (R.N.) Battalion M.G.C. du LE QUESNOYE or relief. Coy. Commander of 63rd Battalion visited Coy. Commanders of 17th. Battalion M.G.C. and arranged relief. Lieut. H.T. DAWE rejoined Battalion from D. Reinforcement Wing and was reappointed Transport Officer.	
	6/5/18		2800 rounds fired on cross roads, communications & targets throughout the night near "C" Coy. Headquarters to BRIGADE Headquarters. "B" Coy. fired up a snipping gun.	

D.W.M.R. Carden
LIEUT. COLONEL,
COMMANDING 17 BATTN. M.G. CORPS.

WAR DIARY
or
INTELLIGENCE SUMMARY.
(Erase heading not required.)

SECRET
17th BATTN.

Place	Date	Hour	Summary of Events and Information	Remarks and references to Appendices
VARENNES	9/5/18		"A" and "C" Coys relieved by two companies of 63rd (R.N.) Battalion. M.G.C. then Bn. rendezvoused at VARENNES and after resting and feeding marched to LE QUESNOYE via HARPONVILLE - TOULENCOURT. "D" Coy. relieved and marched to LE QUESNOYE. 10 signallers joined Battalion from 7th Division.	
LE QUESNOYE	9/5/18		"B" Coy. relieved by a company of 63rd (R.N.) Battalion M.G.C. the Coy. halted at VARENNES for rest and food, and then marched to LE QUESNOYE. Battalion Headquarters moved to LE QUESNOYE opening there at 10 p.m. Conference of Coy. Commanders held at Battalion Headquarters later in event of enemy attack. "D" Coy. again garrisoned Battalion from Divisional wing.	
	10/5/18		LIEUT. J.A. UNDERWOOD 2/Lieut N. AMIS 2/Lieut H.F. MORRELL 2/Lieut. J.C. JENKINS to R.	

Ralph Breeze
LIEUT. COLONEL
COMMANDING 17 BATTN. M.G. CORPS.

WAR DIARY
or
INTELLIGENCE SUMMARY.

SECRET.

17th BATTN. M.G.C.

Army Form C. 2118.

Place	Date	Hour	Summary of Events and Information	Remarks and references to Appendices
LE QUESNOYE	15/5/18		63rd (R.N) M.G. Battalion football team played Battalion team on ground LE QUESNOYE. Result, 2 goals to nil.	
	16/5/18	11.30 a.m.	Battalion was inspected, along with other Divisional troops at V. Corps. HQrs. grounds, Major General C.D. SHUTE, C.B. CMG. After inspection the G.O.C. commanders presented medal ribbons to recipients of MILITARY MEDALS. One O.R. received certificate of gallantry and Devotion to Duty from G.O.C. 17th Division.	
	17/5/18	3.10 p.m.	Sports commenced. Owing to a severe hail storm Battalion Sports forecoded mult and completed Battalion Sports from Divisional Wing.	
	18/5/18		Lt. G.H. MILLS & 2/Lt. H. WOOD & "A" Coy. attached to 50th Brigade for tactical Scheme.	
	19/5/18		Lt. C. WRIGHT and 2/Lt. J.A. WILBY evacuated sick. 17th Battn. M.G.C. and Lancaster Regt. team played Battalion football team on Battn. football ground, winning by 3 goals to nil.	
	20/5/18			

David B Baines
LIEUT. COLONEL
COMMANDING 17 BATTN. M.G. CORPS.

Army Form C. 2118.

WAR DIARY
or
INTELLIGENCE SUMMARY.

SECRET

7th BATTN. M.G.C.

(Erase heading not required.)

Instructions regarding War Diaries and Intelligence Summaries are contained in F.S. Regs., Part II. and the Staff Manual respectively. Title pages will be prepared in manuscript.

Place	Date	Hour	Summary of Events and Information	Remarks and references to Appendices
LE QUESNOYE	21/5/18		1 O.R. "C" Coy. accidentally wounded. 40 O.R. joined from Base Depot.	
	22/5/18		Lieut. Col. D.B. CALDER visited 12th Battalion M.G.C. at ACHEUX to relieve.	
	23/5/18		Lieut. Col. D.B. CALDER visited 12th and 63rd Battalions M.G.C. with regard to arrangements for executing raid with M.G. Barrage. Coy. Commanders visited 12th Battalion M.G.C. re relief. T.D. Coy. marched to BEAUSSART and were attached to 12th Battn. (M.L.G.) for fourteen days. 20 O.R. joined from Base Depot. "B" Coy. marched to VATTENNES and were attached to 63rd (R.N.) M.G. Battalion to assist in raid.	
	24/5/18		"B" & "D" Coys. fired 169,000 rounds for Barrage in connection with combined raid of the 12th and 63rd (R.N.) Divisions into the enemy lines by 2/4th N.A.M.S. evacuated sick	

Anwr B Blase—
LIEUT COLONEL
COMMANDING 7" BATTN. M.G.C.

WAR DIARY or INTELLIGENCE SUMMARY

SECRET. 17th BATTN M.G.

(Erase heading not required.)

Army Form C. 2118.

Place	Date	Hour	Summary of Events and Information	Remarks and references to Appendices
LE QUESNOY	25/5/18		After locating in Rue – "B" Coy went into billets at VARENNES. "D" Coy. went into billets in MAILLY MAILLET. and O.C. Coys made arrangements about Rations with 12th Battalion M.G.C. Lieut Col. R. OAKLEY and Second in Command of 12th Battalion M.G.C. visited Battalion Headquarters.	
ACHEUX.	26/5/18		"A" Coy. relieved Coy. of 12th Battalion M.G.C. in the Left Sector with "A" Coy and "C" Coy marched to ACHEUX and later "A" Coy (½) "B" Coy. relieved 15 Corps of 12th Battn. M.G.C. in the PURPLE LINE. "B" Coy. att'd to ACHEUX at VARENNES. Battalion Headquarters moved to ACHEUX, and opened there at 5 p.m. 4,000 rounds fired on various targets. I.O.R. "A" Coy. wounded in Action. Letters of appreciation received upon the assistance given from 12th and 63rd Battalions by Battalion the test period the Battalion and four hours Running every morning and had sports each afternoon and evening. Lectures in the evening.	

LIEUT.COLONEL,
COMMANDING 17 BATTN. M.G. CORPS.

WAR DIARY or INTELLIGENCE SUMMARY

Army Form C. 2118.

SECRET
17th BATTN. M.G. CORPS

Place	Date	Hour	Summary of Events and Information	Remarks and references to Appendices
ACHEUX	27/5/18		"B" Coy. relieved by 2 of 12th Battalion M.G.C. in the RIGHT SECTOR. 5.O.R. "C" Coy. 12.O.R. "A" Coy. gassed. Lieut. REYNOLDS. "A" Coy. strained. "D" Coy. Headquarters moved to Left Brigade Headquarters. 250 rounds fired at E.A.	
	28/5/18		3650 rounds fired on various targets. Coy. of Ammunition received by 17th Battalion from X Corps. X Corps. C.X. 3491. 27th May 1918. The Corps Commander wishes me to convey to you & Companies of 17th Machine Gun Battalion in subject of the excellent work done by the 12th and 63rd Divisions on the night 24/25th May. Men who took part in the raids have been unanimous in acknowledging the fine support afforded them by our Machine Guns. (Sgd) J.H.C. Sherman Bt Col to D.G.S. Corps.	

LIEUT. COLONEL,
COMMANDING 17 BATTN. M.G. CORPS.

Army Form C. 2118.

WAR DIARY
or
INTELLIGENCE SUMMARY.
(Erase heading not required.)

SECRET.
17th BATTN. M.G.C.

Instructions regarding War Diaries and Intelligence Summaries are contained in F. S. Regs., Part II. and the Staff Manual respectively. Title pages will be prepared in manuscript.

Place	Date	Hour	Summary of Events and Information	Remarks and references to Appendices
ACHEUX	29/5/18		Rounds fired 12,950 on usual targets.	
	30/5/18		Rounds fired 19,000 are taken as place of enemy activity. All M.G. personnel in MAILLY MAILLET moved out of village with order to carry out movement with RIGHT BRIGADE in event of enemy advance. "B" Coy. Headquarters moved to P.17.e.95.80. "C" Coy. Headquarters moved to P.17.e.95.80. All S.O.S. guns fired on Barrage lines in support of attack by 63rd (R.N.) Division. Naval harassing fire programme carried out. Rounds fired I.O.R."A" Coy. 46,750. I.O.R."B" Coy. I.O.R."13" Coy. I.O.R."C" Coy. actual (approx) wounded in Battalion. Strength of Battalion 42 Officers 830 Other ranks	
	31/5/18			

David B Allen
LIEUT. COLONEL
COMMANDING 17 BATTN. M.G. CORPS

SECRET.

17th. Battalion, M.G.C.

5th. July 1918.

F.A. 156.

To. 17th. Division.

Herewith, War Diary of this unit for the month of June.

R.G. Kinsey

Major,
Commanding 17th. Battalion, M.G.C.

Army Form C. 2118.

WAR DIARY
or
INTELLIGENCE SUMMARY.
(Erase heading not required.)

SECRET.

Confidential.

WAR DIARY

OF

17th BATTALION M.G. CORPS

From 1.vi.1918 to 30.vi.1918

Army Form C. 2118.

SECRET

17th Bn M.G.C.

WAR DIARY
or
INTELLIGENCE SUMMARY.

(Erase heading not required.)

Instructions regarding War Diaries and Intelligence Summaries are contained in F. S. Regs., Part II. and the Staff Manual respectively. Title pages will be prepared in manuscript.

Place	Date	Hour	Summary of Events and Information	Remarks and references to Appendices
AIHEUX	1.VI.18		Strength of Battalion :- 42 Officers, 830 O.R.	R.G.K.
			Ordinary indirect fire 14,500 rounds	
			Anti-aircraft fire 250 "	
			4 O.R. "C" Coy wounded (gas), 1 OR "D" Coy wounded	
"	2.VI.18		Ordinary indirect fire 16,000 rounds	R.G.K.
			Anti-aircraft fire 250 "	
			Major J.S. Gowring, O.C. "C" Coy, proceeded on leave to U.K. from 4.VI.18 to 18.VI.18 - this being his first ordinary leave allotted to the Battalion since March 21st	
			3 O.R. "C" Coy wounded (gas), 1 O.R. "B" Coy wounded (accidentally), 1 O.R. "C" Coy wounded	
"	3.VI.18		Ordinary indirect fire 8,750 rounds	R.G.K.
			Anti aircraft fire 100 "	
			S.O.S. 22,750 "	
			At 2.25 A.M. night of 3/4 th June S.O.S signal was sent up on Right Brigade front + guns of "B" Coy at once put down M.G. barrage. O.C. "B" Coy reported O.C. Duke of Wellingtons + Manchester Reg ts have both written to Brigade complimenting the M.G.S. on the rapid way in which they got their guns (guns?) in which

D. D. & I.L. London, E.C.
(A8104) Wt W1771/M2031 750,000 5/W Sch. 53 Forms/C2116/14

WAR DIARY or INTELLIGENCE SUMMARY

Army Form C. 2118.
SECRET.
17th Bn M.G.C.

Place	Date	Hour	Summary of Events and Information	Remarks and references to Appendices
ACHEUX	3/6/18 (contd)		fire was maintained. O.C. Manchester Regt. is of the opinion that it was due to the M.G's that the attack on his front did not develop. 2 OR "B" Coy. killed; 1 OR "B" Coy wounded; 1 OR "B" Coy wounded at duty; 1 OR "D" Coy wounded. Harassing indirect fire — 9,500 rounds. Anti-aircraft fire — 200 " . Snipping gun fired upon by "D" Coy near AUCHONVILLERS left sector. 1 OR "C" Coy wounded; 1 OR "D" wounded accidentally	R.S.K.
"	4/6/18		Harassing indirect fire — 8,000 rounds. Anti-aircraft fire — 100 " . "A" Coy. relieved "B" Coy in the RIGHT SECTOR, two sections of "B" withdrawing to ACHEUX + two to the PURPLE LINE where they came under the command of "A" Coy. 2nd Lieut. Birch "A" Coy. proceeded on special leave to U.K. from 7.4.18 to 21.4.18. 1 OR "A" Coy wounded; 1 OR "A" Coy wounded (gas); 1 OR "D" Coy wounded	R.S.K.
"	5/6/18			R.S.K.

SECRET

Army Form C. 2118.

WAR DIARY
or
INTELLIGENCE SUMMARY.
(Erase heading not required.)

17th Bn M.G.C.

Place	Date	Hour	Summary of Events and Information	Remarks and references to Appendices
ACHEUX	6.VI.18		Desultory indirect fire 11,300 rounds. "C" Coy relieved "D" Coy in the LEFT SECTOR, the whole of the latter Coys subsequently proceeding to positions in the PURPLE LINE vacated by "C" Coy. The two Platoons of "B" Coy coming under the command of O.C. "D" Coy. Major Hough, O.C. "B" Coy, is awarded the Military Cross by H.M. The King. — London Gazette 3.VI.1918. Two Coys 63rd R.N. Div. came under the control of the Bn to take up Battery positions preparatory to the front passed over the 8th inst. 1 OR "A" Coy wounded.	R.G.K.
"	7.VI.18		Desultory indirect fire 15,080 rounds. Lieut G.H. Mills "C" Coy is awarded the Military Cross by H.M. The King. Gazette 3.VI.1918. Nothing other.	R.G.K.
"	8.VI.18		Desultory harassing fire Nil. Special barrage fire 275, 250 rounds. During the night a minor operation was carried out by the 53rd Bgde to which our guns lent effective support. Two platoons of "D" Coy moved into position the previous	R.G.K.

WAR DIARY
INTELLIGENCE SUMMARY

Army Form C. 2118.

SECRET

17th Bn M.G.C.

Place	Date	Hour	Summary of Events and Information	Remarks and references to Appendices
ACHEUX	8.VI.18 (contd.)		PURPLE LINE – tiro action of "B" Coy from ACHEUX is to operate with guns of "A" Coys in RIGHT & LEFT SECTORS respectively. These fire tasks referred to their normal positions as soon as the operation was completed. Assembly was also given by guns of 42nd, 63rd & 38th 18th M.G. Coys. 2nd Lieut A.S. Belding "B" Coy wounded & remained at duty. 2 F.R. "B" Coy wounded. 1 F.R. "A" Coy wounded (gas)	R.S.R.
	9.VI.18		Unusual machine gun fire. 16,750 rounds. T 2nd Lieut A.W. Higgins "B" Coy to K.T. Lieut from 25.V.18 - London Gazette 5.VI.18. 1 O.R. "D" Coy Killed, 1 O.R. "D" Coy wounded accidentally.	R.S.R.
	10.VI.18		Ordinary indirect fire 14,750 rounds. Anti aircraft fire 750 ". During the morning Brigadier General L. Wigan Thomas D.S.O. commanding 50 R. Inf. Bde. (subject to approval of the M.G. Barrage in support of operation on the 8th inst. to morning conveying his words "well done" to the 63rd (R.N.) 38th & 42nd Divs. Capt. Adjt. A.M.Gwen proceeded on leave to U.K. from 12.VI.18 – 26.VI.18 his place being taken by 2nd Lieut. F.H. Arnold, Intelligence Officer. 2 F.R. "D" Adin promoted in field. No casualties.	R.S.R.

Army Form C. 2118.

SECRET
17th Bn M.G.C.

WAR DIARY
or
INTELLIGENCE SUMMARY.
(Erase heading not required.)

Instructions regarding War Diaries and Intelligence Summaries are contained in F. S. Regs., Part II. and the Staff Manual respectively. Title pages will be prepared in manuscript.

Place	Date	Hour	Summary of Events and Information	Remarks and references to Appendices
ACHEUX	11.VI.18		Unloading indirect fire 16,100 rounds. Ammunition fired 150 " No 3556 Sergt Platt M. A copy is annexed of the D.C.M. London Gazette L.VI.18. Following letter was received from the Hon. Treasurer of the M.G Banners of War Fund :- "With your picture accept the thanks of my Committee for your very generous help in aid of the fund. The cheque value £66-12-7" Note that M.G rounds of the Battalion under your command have kindly agreed to give in monthly intimation for decision which is very much appreciated. No casualties	R.S.R.
	12.VI.18		Ordinary indirect fire 15,500 rounds The following appeared in orders :- "The G.O.C of the Infantry Brigade which carried one the successful raid on the night of 8/9.VI.18 has personally expressed his appreciation of the valuable assistance rendered by the Machine Guns during the operations. The Infantry, who took part in the raid state that the M.G barrage was splendid (That the way it was maintained inspired them with confidence) 2nd Lieut T.W Abernethy } joined the Batt from Div Wing C. Lindop } on reinforcements Major A.R.Fraser } proceeded to U.K on duty Lieut. H.T Davy } under the Six months W.S Tanner } Substitution Scheme	R.S.R.

Army Form C. 2118.

SECRET
17th Bn M.G.C.

WAR DIARY
or
INTELLIGENCE SUMMARY.
(Erase heading not required.)

Place	Date	Hour	Summary of Events and Information	Remarks and references to Appendices
ACHEUX	12.VI.18 (contd:)		2Lieut. W.E.G. Jones "C" Coy. and 2nd Div. Wing, proceeded to D.R. on duty	R.G.R.
			2.1 O.R. rejoined from Div. Wing	
			45 O.R. joined from Div. Wing as reinforcements.	
			2 O.R. "C" Coy wounded ; 1 O.R. "C" Coy wounded (gas)	
			Lieut. S. Henry "A" Coy admitted to hospital sick & evacuated from Corps Area.	
	13.VI.18		Ordinary indirect fire 14,000 rounds.	R.G.R.
			"D" Coy relieved "A" Coy in the RIGHT SECTOR the whole of the latter Coy subsequently proceeding to positions in the PURPLE LINE vacated by "D" Coy, the light guns of "B" Coy coming under the commands of O.C. "A" Coy.	
			2 Lieut. T. Ramshorn } joined the Batt. from Div. Wing as reinforcements	
			G.F. Reid }	
			44 O.R. joined from Div. Wing as reinforcements	
			1 O.R. "A" Coy wounded	
	14.VI.18		Ordinary indirect fire 7000 rounds	R.G.R.
			"B" Coy relieved "C" Coy in the LEFT SECTOR, two sections of "C" Coy withdrawing to ACHEUX Two to the PURPLE LINE where they came under the commands of O.C. "A" Coy	
			1 O.R. "C" Coy wounded	

Army Form C. 2118.

SECRET

17th Bn MGC

WAR DIARY or INTELLIGENCE SUMMARY

(Erase heading not required.)

Instructions regarding War Diaries and Intelligence Summaries are contained in F.S. Regs., Part II. and the Staff Manual respectively. Title pages will be prepared in manuscript.

Place	Date	Hour	Summary of Events and Information	Remarks and references to Appendices
ACHEUX	15.vi.18		Ordinary indirect fire. 15,000 rounds. On this date the following order appeared in Bntt orders :— "A prize of 100 francs (out of C.O's fund) will be awarded at the end of each month to the Coy which has the best salvage return for the month. A record of salvage collected by each Coy will be published. The disposal of the 100 francs is left to the Discretion of the Coy Commanders regarding the proportion of prize amongst sections." 1 OR "A" Coy, 1 OR "B" Coy proceeded on leave to UK Casualties — Nil.	R.S.K.
	16.vi.18		Ordinary indirect fire . 13,150 rounds A F.G.C.M. was held at the ECOLE COMMUNALE des FILLES, ACHEUX at which the O.R of the Battn. was tried & truly acquitted. Major E.W. Davis, OC "A" Coy, acted as prosecutors friend. Casualties — Nil. "B" Coy Hqrs moved to Left Brigade Hqrs.	R.S.K.
	17.vi.18		Ordinary indirect fire. 17,100 rounds 255 rounds fired by left Sector sniping guns which engaged 10 targets during the day with satisfactory results Casualties. Nil.	R.S.K.

Army Form C. 2118.

SECRET.

17th Bn M.G.C.

WAR DIARY
or
INTELLIGENCE SUMMARY.

(Erase heading not required.)

Place	Date	Hour	Summary of Events and Information	Remarks and references to Appendices
ACHEUX	18.vi.18		Desultory indirect fire - 16,500 rounds. Anti-aircraft " 70 " "B" Coy had one gun completely knocked out. 2 Lieut. I.C. Jenkins "B" Coy wounded. 1 O.R. "B" Coy killed; 2 O.R. "B" Coy wounded. 1 O.R. "D" Coy wounded + remained at duty. "D" Coy H.Qrs moved to Right Brigade H.Qrs. Left Section Supply Gun engaged two targets; 55 rounds were fired + enemy was seen to scatter.	R.S.R.
	19.vi.18		Desultory indirect fire 3,900 rounds Special " " 20,000 " Anti-aircraft " 75 " During the night all available guns of "B" + "D" Coys fired on special targets in connection with the simultaneous discharge of 600 gas projectors by a Special R.E. Coy + a feint attack by the 38th Div. on AVELUY WOOD. No 3281 Sgt. Peacock E.M. "D" Coy mentioned in Despatches - London Gazette 25.v.18 2 Lieut A.W. Wellings D.C.M. "A" Coy wounded. Major J.S. Gowring o.c. "C" Coy returned from leave. 1 O.R. "A" Coy, 1 O.R. "D" Coy proceeded on leave to U.K.	R.915.

SECRET

Army Form C. 2118.

WAR DIARY
INTELLIGENCE SUMMARY

17th Bn M.G.C

(Erase heading not required.)

Place	Date	Hour	Summary of Events and Information	Remarks and references to Appendices
ACHEUX	20.VI.18		Ordinary indirect fire 9,270 rounds Special barrage fire 58,000 " Left Sector sniping gun fired on a small party of the enemy + scattered them. In the night of 20/21 June a raid was made by the 38th Div. north of AVELUY WOOD. This battalion co-operated with two 8-gun batteries - "K" battery consisted of 8 guns of "A" Coy which moved up from the PURPLE LINE for the operation into positions specially prepared the previous night + returned to their normal positions as soon as it was completed. "L" battery consisted of 8 guns of "D" Coy, occupying the RIGHT SECTOR Units tests from their normal night-firing positions. Lt (A. McCready, 63rd Bn (R.N.D) M.G.C. visited H.Q. respecting forthcoming relief.	R.S.K.
"	21.VI.18		Ordinary indirect fire 12,660 rounds Anti-aircraft fire 200 " Left Sector sniping gun scored six hits. Coy Commander of 63rd Bn M.G.C. visited Coy Commanders of this battalion preparatory to taking over. Lieut W.B. Martin } joined Batt. from Div. Wing and were posted 2 Lieut F.J. Eldridge } to "A" + "D" Coys respectively.	R.S.K.

WAR DIARY or INTELLIGENCE SUMMARY

Army Form C. 2118.

SECRET

17th Bn MGC

Place	Date	Hour	Summary of Events and Information	Remarks and references to Appendices
ACHEUX	22.vi.18		Ordinary indirect fire 6,040 rounds. Lt. Col. Mihradi 63rd Bn. (RND) MGC went round the line with Major Kinsey, M.C. D. Coy was relieved by "C" Coy 63rd Bn in the Right Sector & after resting in ACHEUX WOOD marched to TOUTENCOURT to rejoin Batt. vacated by MG relieving Coy.	R.S.K.
"	23.vi.18		Battalion HQ closed at ACHEUX at 9.0 AM re-opening at TOUTENCOURT at the same time. "A" Coy with two sections of "C" Coy was relieved in the PURPLE LINE by "A" Coy with two sections of "B" Coy, 63rd Bn. marching to TOUTENCOURT on relief. B Echelons of all Coy's proceeded to TOUTENCOURT with "C" Coy less two sections under Major Gowring. "B" Coy was relieved by "D" Coy 63rd Bn in the LEFT SECTOR & after resting in ACHEUX WOOD marched to TOUTENCOURT to occupy billets vacated by the relieving Coy. Capt. P.G. Fry joined the Batt. from Div. Wing & was posted to "D" Coy of which he assumed Command.	R.S.K.
TOUTENCOURT				
"	24.vi.18		2.Lieut. H.G. Hutcham joined the Batt. ex Div. Wing & was posted to "C" Coy. On this date all personnel previously posted & attached to Batt. Hqrs became "Headquarters Coy" A.G.R. for the purposes of discipline rations & pay. Strength of this Coy was then as follows:— Posted 68 AM & 26 19 O.R. arrived from Div. Wing as reinforcements	

Army Form C. 2118.

SECRET
17th 13th MGC

WAR DIARY
or
INTELLIGENCE SUMMARY.
(Erase heading not required.)

Instructions regarding War Diaries and Intelligence Summaries are contained in F. S. Regs., Part II. and the Staff Manual respectively. Title pages will be prepared in manuscript.

Place	Date	Hour	Summary of Events and Information	Remarks and references to Appendices
TOUTENCOURT	25.vi.18		On this date & many succeeding days an epidemic of Influenza caused very high sick parades. Practically all who were treated in billets. Precautions were taken to the limits of infection.	R.G.K.
			Major R.G. Kinzey M.C assumed command. Coy Commander nominated BROWN & PURPLE LINES. Each Coy detailed 1 Officer, 8 O.R & 2 guns i/c for duty as a mobile section in the event of transfer of Div to XXII Corps while in G.H.Q reserve.	
"	26.vi.18		Lieut. Col: D.B Calder proceeded on leave to U.K from 27.vi.18 to 11.vii.18. Special billets were set aside for Officers & O.R of the Mobile section so that no time would be lost in the event of an emergency call.	R.G.R.
"	27.vi.18		Lieut G.H Mills M.C "C" Coy admitted to hospital sick while on course at I Corps Gas School. 1 O.R proceeded to U.K - candidate for Commission	R.S.M.
"	28.vi.18		Lieut Perch "A" Coy returned from leave. Major Kinsey visited Hqrs 12th 13th MGC respecting forthcoming operations by 12th & 18th Divisions for which co-operation by our guns had to be arranged.	R.S.M.

SECRET
17th Bn M.G.C.

Army Form C. 2118.

WAR DIARY or INTELLIGENCE SUMMARY.

(Erase heading not required.)

Place	Date	Hour	Summary of Events and Information	Remarks and references to Appendices
TOUTENCOURT	29/6/18		During night of 29/30 June each Coy. sent into the line in the neighbourhood of MARTINSART two 8-gun batteries for the purpose of assisting operations already referred to. Personnel of these batteries travelled by lorry from TOUTENCOURT to a point on the BOUZINCOURT - SENLIS road. 2/Lt. E.G. Mungeam "C" Coy. admitted to hospital sick.	R.S.R.
"	30/6/18		Rounds fired during 12th Div. operations & subsequent enemy counter attack:- BARRAGE S.O.S A Coy 112,000 78,000 B " 96,000 64,000 C " 110,000 50,000 D " 96,000 24,000 420,000 216,000 Total Rounds:- 636,000 2 D.R. "B" Coy. Killed. Capt. J.S. Walker "B" Coy. admitted to hospital sick. STRENGTH OF BATTALION Officers O.R. 43 884	R.S.R.

R.S.Kincey
Major
Comdg. 17 Bn M.G.C.

SECRET.

17th Battalion, M.G.C.

3rd August.1918.

To:- H.Q. 17th Division.   G.111.

"G".

Herewith War Diary of this Unit for the
month of July.

Lieut-Colonel,
Commanding 17th Battalion.M.G.

Army Form C. 2118.

WAR DIARY
or
INTELLIGENCE SUMMARY.
(Erase heading not required.)

SECRET

Confidential

WAR DIARY

OF

17th BATTALION M.G. CORPS

From 1. vii. 1918 to 31. vii. 1918

Instructions regarding War Diaries and Intelligence Summaries are contained in F. S. Regs., Part II. and the Staff Manual respectively. Title pages will be prepared in manuscript.

Place	Date	Hour	Summary of Events and Information	Remarks and references to Appendices

Army Form C. 2118.

WAR DIARY
or
INTELLIGENCE SUMMARY
(Erase heading not required.)

SECRET.

Place	Date	Hour	Summary of Events and Information	Remarks and references to Appendices
TOUTENCOURT.	July 1st. 1918.		Strength of Battalion :- 43 Officers, 884 Other Ranks. At 2.0.a.m. one battery of "D" Company, withdrew, having finished firing in connection with operations of 12th Division, and personnel returned to TOUTENCOURT in lorries. This battery then took over duties of Mobile Section. At dusk, one battery of "B" Company, and remaining battery of "D" Coy, withdrew, personnel returning to TOUTENCOURT in lorries. Remaining batteries were retained in position owing to the tactical situation. 2/Lieut.G.T.Fraser joined the Battalion from Base Depot, and was posted to "B" Coy. 4 - O.R. "A" Coy, Wounded; 2 - O.R. "C" Coy, Wounded; 3 - O.R. "C" Coy, Wounded,(gas).	

TOUTENCOURT.	July 2nd.		During night 2nd/3rd July, remaining batteries,viz,-one of "B" Coy;two of "A" Coy, and two of "C" Coy, were withdrawn, personnel returning to TOUTENCOURT in lorries. Following appeared in orders:- Result of Competition for Salvage for the Month of June in connection with prize of 100 Francs to best Coy. in Salvage return:-
			
			    1st. "B" Coy. £596. -- 6.
			    2nd. "A" " £473. 16. 11½
			    3rd. "D" " £423. 9. 4.
			    4th. "C" " £300. 15. 6¾
			
			    Total. £1,794. 2. 4¼.
			
			Capt. & Adjt. A.McInnes. returned from Leave. 1 - O.R.Granted leave to U.K. (cont'd)	

D.M.Bailey
LIEUT. COLONEL
COMMANDING 17 BATTN. M.G. CORPS.

Army Form C. 2118.

WAR DIARY
or
INTELLIGENCE SUMMARY.

(Erase heading not required.)

SECRET.

Instructions regarding War Diaries and Intelligence Summaries are contained in F.S. Regs., Part II. and the Staff Manual respectively. Title pages will be prepared in manuscript.

Place	Date	Hour	Summary of Events and Information	Remarks and references to Appendices
TOUTENCOURT.	July 2nd.		3 - O.R.Leave to Paris; 4 - O.R. "A" Coy, wounded; 2 - O.R. "A" Coy, wounded (Gas).	
TOUTENCOURT.	July 3rd.		2/Lieut.A.C.Wylde joined the Battalion from Base Depot, and was posted to "C" Coy. 1 - O.R.proceeded to U.K. on leave.	
TOUTENCOURT.	July 4th.		The Battalion was visited by G.S.O. I. who inspected each Company at training. A commencement was made by the Corps Eyepiece Factory with the fitting of New Triplex -glass eyepieces in our respirators. This work was continued on the 5th and 6th inst.	
TOUTENCOURT.	July 5th.		Each Company had firing practice on the long range at LE QUESNOIE FARM, near PUCHEVILLERS during the 4th, 5th, and 6th inst. The firing was combined with small tactical schemes.	
TOUTENCOURT.	July 6th.		Battalion paraded for Divine Service under the command of Major E.W.Davis, O.C."A" Coy. Major.R.G.Kinsey.M.C, visited H.Q.12th Battalion M.G.C near HARPONVILLE, respecting forthcoming relief.	
TOUTENCOURT.	July 7th.		"Practice Stand-to" orders were received at 11.30 p.m. followed by orders to "Practice take up Assembly positions". After all Companies had moved off, Major Kinsey proceeded to a point near HARPONVILLE, where Bn.H.Q. were established at 2.15 a.m. 8th inst. "A" & "B" Coys reached their Assembly positions at 2.35 a.m. "C" Coy, was in position in the BROWN LINE by 3.40 a.m. and "D" Coy, by 4.0 a.m. "Practice Ended" message was received at 6.0 a.m. and Battalion then returned to billets.	

David B Davis
LIEUT. COLONEL,
COMMANDING 17 BATTN. M.G. CORPS

Army Form C. 2118.

WAR DIARY
or
INTELLIGENCE SUMMARY

(Erase heading not required.)

SECRET.

Place	Date	Hour	Summary of Events and Information	Remarks and references to Appendices
TOUTENCOURT.	July 8th. 1918.		Lieut-Colonel Oakley, and Major Caddick Adams, 12th Battalion. M.G.C, visited Major Kinsey respecting relief. Company Commanders visited 12th Battalion M.G.C. Company Commanders in the line, to make the necessary arrangements for relief of Companies.	
TOUTENCOURT.	July 9th.		Major Kinsey went round the line with Lt-Col.Oakley. "C" Coy, with two Sections of "A" Coy, relieved "B" Coy, 12th Battalion, M.G.C and 2 sections of "C" Coy. 12th Battalion.M.G.C.	
TOUTENCOURT HARPONVILLE. (U.11.d.O.2.)	July 10th.		"B" Coy. relieved "A" Coy.12th Bn.M.G.C. "B" Coy, with 2 sections of "A" Coy, relieved "D" Coy.12th Bn.M.G.C.and 2 sections of "C" Coy,12th Bn.M.G.C. Battalion Headquarters closed at TOUTENCOURT at 5.0.p.m. re-opening at HARPONVILLE U.11.d.O.2. at the same hour. Rounds fired, - Ordinary Indirect fire, - 6000 rounds. Extract from Part I Orders:- The following sum has today been despatched to the Hon.Treas.P.of W.Fund, M.G.T.C.Grantham. "H.Q" Coy.....100 Francs. "A" " ....334 " "B" " ....216 " "C" " ....238 " "D" " ....207 " Total.....1,103 Subscribed for by Officers, W.O's, N.C.O's and men for month of June.	
	July 11th.		Ordinary Indirect fire, - 7,500 rounds fired. (cont'd)	

David R……
LIEUT. COLONEL
COMMANDING 17 BATTn. M.G. CORPS.

Army Form C. 2118.

WAR DIARY
or
INTELLIGENCE SUMMARY

S E C R E T.

(Erase heading not required.)

Place	Date	Hour	Summary of Events and Information	Remarks and references to Appendices
HARPONVILLE.	July 11th 1918.		Major Kinsey visited O's.C. "A" & "C" Coys; in the line. Lieut.G.S.M.Morgan joined Battalion from Base Depot, and was posted to "A" Coy. 2/Lieut.E.G.MUngeam "C" Coy, rejoined ex Base Depot. 2/Lieut.D.G.Latimer joined Battalion ex Base Depot, and was posted to "B" Coy. 3 - O.R. joined Battalion, as reinforcements, ex Div.Wing.	
HARPONVILLE.	July 12th.		Ordinary indirect fire, - 16,250 rounds. Lieut-Colonel.D.B.Calder returned from Leave, resuming Command of the Battalion on the 13th inst.	
HARPONVILLE.	July 13th.		Ordinary indirect fire, - 21,340 rounds. On this day, the first Sergeant from the Army Veterinary Corps, recently added to the establishment, joined the Battalion. 1 - O.R. "C" Coy, proceeded to U.K. - candidate for Commission.	
HARPONVILLE.	July 14th.		Ordinary indirect fire, - 20,000 rounds. A.A.fire - 270 rounds. 2/Lieut.D.Lindop, "D" Coy., evacuated out of Corps Area. 1 - O.R.proceeded to U.K. on Leave.	
HARPONVILLE.	July 15th.		Ordinary indirect fire, 18,550.rounds. On this date it was arranged that in future our indirect night firing, would, as far as possible, be directed against targets engaged by Field Artillery, in accordance with the programme sent us daily by Division.	

David B Calder
LIEUT. COLONEL.
COMMANDING 17 BATTN. M.G. CORPS.

Army Form C. 2118.

WAR DIARY
or
INTELLIGENCE SUMMARY

SECRET.

(Erase heading not required.)

Instructions regarding War Diaries and Intelligence Summaries are contained in F. S. Regs., Part II and the Staff Manual respectively. Title pages will be prepared in manuscript.

Place	Date	Hour	Summary of Events and Information	Remarks and references to Appendices
HARPONVILLE.	July 16th. 1918.		Ordinary indirect fire, - 20,800 rounds. A.A.fire 300 rounds. Lieut-Colonel D.B.Calder visited Divisional H.Q. in connection with the forthcoming adjustment of the front caused by the withdrawal of the 38th Division from the line, and subsequent holding of the V Corps front with two Divisions.	
HARPONVILLE.	July 17th.		Ordinary indirect fire, - 20,000 rounds, A.A.Fire. - 130 rds. Lieut-Colonel D.B.Calder visited Lieut-Colonel Lyttleton, Commanding 38th Battalion, M.G.C. to make arrangements for taking over Right Sector guns of Centre Division on night 19th/20th July.	
HARPONVILLE.	July 18th.		Ordinary indirect fire, - 13,000 rounds. During the night M.G.adjustments of the new Divisional front were made as follows:- (i). Guns of "C" Coy, took over positions in the Right Brigade Sector. (ii). Guns of "B" Coy. took over M.G.positions in the Centre Brigade Sector. (iii). Six guns of "A" Coy. took over positions in the PURPLE LINE and the remaining 10 withdrew to BROWN LINE at V.3.b.25.25. (iv). Two guns of "D" Coy. took over positions of "B" Coy in the New Left Brigade Sector. 2/Lieut. G.F.Reid, "A" Coy, wounded in action. 1. O.R. "A" Coy, wounded and remained at Duty.	
HARPONVILLE. FORCEVILLE. F.27.b.1.2.	July 19th.		Ordinary indirect fire - 18,000 rounds. AA.fire.- 350 rounds. During the night, "D" Coy relieved 14 guns of 38th Bn.M.G.C. in Right Sector of	

David Bell
LIEUT. COLONEL
COMMANDING 17 BATTN. M.G. CORPS.

WAR DIARY
INTELLIGENCE SUMMARY

(Erase heading not required.)

Army Form C. 2118.

S E C R E T .

Place	Date	Hour	Summary of Events and Information	Remarks and references to Appendices
FORCEVILLE.	July 19th contd.		Centre Division, which now became AVELUI LEFT, or Left Brigade Sector, Right Division. 2 guns of "A" Coy took over from the 38th Battalion M.G.C. in the PURPLE LINE. Battalion H.Q. closed at HARPONVILLE at noon re-opening at the same hour at FORCEVILLE, (F.27.b.1.2) Transport and "B" Echelon removed to 0.36.b.&.d.(VARENNES) 1 O.R. "D" Coy proceeded to U.K. candidate for commission. Ordinary indirect fire. - 23,750. rounds. A.A.Fire - 50 rounds. 4 - O.R.joined Battalion as reinforcements, ex Divisional Wing. 2 - O.R. joined ex Div.Wing.	
FORCEVILLE.	July 20th.		Ordinary indirect fire, 33,500 rounds. A.A.Fire 150 rounds. On this date our Night firing programme was considerably increased, a captured prisoner having stated that a relief was taking place. 4 - O.R. rejoined ex Hospital.	
FORCEVILLE.	July 21st.		Ordinary indirect fire, 25,700.rounds. A.A.Fire 765 rounds. A F.G.C.M. was held at ECOLE des FILLES, HARPONVILLE, - President Major H.B.Lees, Westmorland & Cumberland Yeomanry, attached 10th Sherwood Foresters, for the trial of No.3573, Sgt Lloyd, D, and 3502, Pte Newse W, both of this Battalion. 2 - O.R.proceeded on leave to U.K. 1 O.R. rejoined ex Hospital. 1 O.R. rejoined ex Div.Wing, 1 O.R. "A" Coy. wounded.	
FORCEVILLE.	July 22nd.			

David Bacon
LIEUT: COLONEL,
COMMANDING 17 BATTN. M.G. CORPS.

Army Form C. 2118.

WAR DIARY
or
INTELLIGENCE SUMMARY.   S E C R E T .
(Erase heading not required)

Instructions regarding War Diaries and Intelligence Summaries are contained in F.S. Regs., Part II. and the Staff Manual respectively. Title pages will be prepared in manuscript.

Place	Date	Hour	Summary of Events and Information	Remarks and references to Appendices
FORCEVILLE.	July 23rd.		Ordinary Indirect fire, - 30,000 rounds. Special Indirect fire, - 7,500 rounds. Our guns fired on enemy Tracks, Roads, and Centres of activity at irregular intervals, from dusk till dawn Intense bursts were fired between midnight and 3.0 a.m. to assist an operation by the 47th Division on our Right. Four guns of "C" Company fired special enfilading fire in connection with this operation. 1 - O.R. "D" Coy. Killed in action, 1 - O.R. "D" Coy wounded. These casualties were the result of a direct hit on a gun position. The gun itself was buried, but not damaged.	
FORCEVILLE.	July 24th.		Ordinary indirect fire 24,000 rounds. A.A.fire. 500 rounds. On this date, 1 G.S.Wagon, and two Water carts complete with animals, arrived to complete establishment. 3 A.S.C.Drivers attached to Battalion from No.3.Army Auxiliary (Horse) Transport Coy. 2 O.R.proceeded on Leave to U.K. 2/Lieut.J.W.Jones, "A" Coy, admitted to Hospital, sick.	
FORCEVILLE.	July 25th.		Ordinary indirect fire, 24,000 rounds, A.A.Fire, 500 rounds. 1 O.R. "C" Coy, wounded and remained at Duty. 2 Drivers joined Battalion as reinforcements ex Adv.H.T.Depot.	
FORCEVILLE.	July 26th.		Ordinary Indirect fire.27,000 rounds. contd.	

David Blade
LIEUT. COLONEL,
COMMANDING 17 BATTN. M.G. CORPS

Army Form C. 2118.

WAR DIARY
or
INTELLIGENCE SUMMARY.   SECRET.

(Erase heading not required.)

Instructions regarding War Diaries and Intelligence Summaries are contained in F. S. Regs., Part II. and the Staff Manual respectively. Title pages will be prepared in manuscript.

Place	Date	Hour	Summary of Events and Information	Remarks and references to Appendices
FROGEVILLE.	July 26th 1918.		"A" Coy.H.Q's. moved from V.3.b.25.25. (off HEDAUVILLE-WARLOY Road) to V.18.a.1.9. (with "C" Coy). Capt.J.S.Walker, "B" Company, previously evacuated sick, rejoined 2Battalion. 2/Lieut.C.E.Gowers, joined Battalion as reinforcement, ex Base Depot, and was posted to "D" Coy. 19 O.R.joined Battalion as reinforcement ex Div.Wing. 1 O.R. rejoined ex Div.Wing.	
FORCEVILLE.	July 27th		Ordinary indirect fire 26,000 rounds. O.C.314th(American) M.G.Bn visited Bn.H.Q. with Major Muller(C.M.G.O.V.Corps) to arrange details of forthcoming instructional tour of his unit and 318th (American) M.G.Coy, in the line, with this battalion. Pte Palframan "C" Coy, won the Divisional Heavyweight Boxing Tournament at HARPONVILLE and became attached to Div.H.Q. to undergo special training for the Corps Championship.	
FORCEVILLE.	July 28th.		Ordinary indirect fire, 25,500 rounds. Our Left Sector Sniping gun engaged four targets. One part of 6 was scattered, and a party of 70 - 100 in AUTHUILLE Village dispersed. During the afternoon the enemy obtained a direct hit on one of "C" Coy's positions, rendering the tripod useless.	

David Blackett
LIEUT. COLONEL
COMMANDING 17 BATTN. M.G. CORPS

Army Form C. 2118.

WAR DIARY
or
INTELLIGENCE SUMMARY

S E C R E T.

(Erase heading not required.)

Instructions regarding War Diaries and Intelligence Summaries are contained in F.S. Regs, Part II. and the Staff Manual respectively. Title pages will be prepared in manuscript.

Place	Date	Hour	Summary of Events and Information	Remarks and references to Appendices
FORCEVILLE.	July 28th contd.		2/Lieut.H.G.Rowles "B" Coy, left for Veterinary Course at Abbeville. Lieut.R.G.Bond.A.S.C. (attached 7th East Yorks Regt) attached to Battalion Transport for duty. 1 O.R. granted leave to U.K. Ordinary Indirect fire, 26,600 rounds.	
FORCEVILLE.	July 29th.		During the afternoon a party of Four American Officers and 44 O.R. reported at H.Q. where they were met by guides and taken to B,C.&D.Coys' H.Q's in the line, for individual instruction by opposite numbers. Lieut.A.Abraham. R.E. attached to H.Q. for duty as Signalling Officer. Ordinary Indirect fire, 34,000 rounds; Special Indirect fire, 52,875 rounds, - total 86,875 rounds.	
FORCEVILLE.	July 30th.		At 9.0.a.m. a Sham Attack was carried out along the Corps Front, and 34 of our guns co-operated with the Artillery, and T.M's. "C" Coy. had one gun blown in but suffered no casualties. During night firing, "D" Coy also had a gun damaged beyond repair. 1 O.R. "C" Coy, wounded and remained at duty. Ordinary indirect fire 30,200 rounds. A further party of American Troops arrived to take the place of those under instruction, the latter party returning to camp at LE QUESNOIE by motor lorry, from Bn.H.Q. Lieut.F.N.S.Darby, Signalling Officer struck off the strength, and posted to No 5.	
FORCEVILLE.	July 31st.			

David B Barley
LIEUT. COLONEL,
COMMANDING 17 BATTN. M.G. CORPS

WAR DIARY
or
INTELLIGENCE SUMMARY

SECRET.

(Erase heading not required.)

Army Form C. 2118.

Instructions regarding War Diaries and Intelligence Summaries are contained in F. S. Regs., Part II. and the Staff Manual respectively. Title pages will be prepared in manuscript.

Place	Date	Hour	Summary of Events and Information	Remarks and references to Appendices
FORCEVILLE.	July 31st, contd		Divisional Signal Coy. 1 O.R. proceeded on leave to U.K.	
			The following is the result of the Salvage competition for the month of July:-	
			1st. "B" Coy. £1,856- 0- 5¼.	
			2nd. " D" " £1,028-19-10¾.	
			3rd. " C" " 598-10-10.	
			4th. " A" " 296- 3- 1¼.	
			Total. £3,779-14- 3¼.	
			Number of Rounds fired during the month:- 648,460.	
			Strength of Battalion:- Officers:- 43.	
			Other Ranks.:- 850.	

David Baden
LIEUT. COLONEL.
COMMANDING 17 BATTN. M.G. CORPS.

17th Divl.
Troops

17th BATTALION

MACHINE GUN CORPS,

AUGUST 1918.

No 24

Secret and Confidential   W 7

War Diary
of
17th Battalion M. G. C.

From 1.8.18 to 31.8.18

Army Form C. 2118.

WAR DIARY
or
INTELLIGENCE SUMMARY
CONFIDENTIAL.
(Erase heading not required.)

Instructions regarding War Diaries and Intelligence Summaries are contained in F.S. Regs., Part II. and the Staff Manual respectively. Title pages will be prepared in manuscript.

Place	Date	Hour	Summary of Events and Information	Remarks and references to Appendices
FORCEVILLE. P.27.b.1.2. Sheet 57d, 1/40,000 & Sheet 57d.S.E. 1/20,000	Aug. 1st. 1918.		AUGUST 1918. Strength of Battalion :- 43 Officers; 850 Other Ranks. Special Barrages fired for Raids...106,850 rounds. Ordinary indirect fire............ 9,000 rounds. Anti-Aircraft................... 600 rounds. During the night raids were carried out by the 50th and 51st Infantry Brigades, 30 of our guns fired in support of the former, and 14 in support of the latter. In addition we obtained the assistance of 8 guns for the former from the 47th Division on our Right. We had no casualties. 2/Lieut.E.J.C.Cubberley, Transport Officer, to be Lieutenant, 2/7/18, - London Gazette 29/7/18. 1.O.R. "D" Coy. proceeded on leave to U.K.	
FORCEVILLE, P.27.b.1.2.	2/8/18.		Ordinary indirect fire, ...9,950 rounds. The enemy commenced his withdrawal to the East of the ANCRE on this day, and our patrols commenced to push forward into the evacuated area. It was therefore necessary to stop all harassing fire. Lt-Col.Lyttleton, Commanding 38th Battalion, M.G.C, visited H.Q. to arrange details of forthcoming relief. A third party of American Troops arrived for a two days tour of individual instruction with our Companies, the second party returning to their unit during the afternoon. 2/Lieut.T.Rawlinson, "B" Coy.) 2/Lieut.R.A.Pleace. "A" ") Left for Musketry Course at 3rd Army School. 2/Lieut.H.G.Holoran. "C" " Left for Infantry Course at 3rd Army School. 1. O.R. "D" Coy. proceeded on Leave to U.K.	
FORCEVILLE. P.27.b.1.2.	3/8/18.		No firing, owing to continued enemy withdrawal. Orders received that no guns will move forward for the present, but that new S.O.S.lines will be arranged for any that can fire East of the ANCRE on the approaches to the river. Safety Clearance over the Western Bank of the river must be allowed for to safeguard our patrols. Only six guns available for firing in compliance with these orders. continued.	

Army Form C. 2118.

WAR DIARY
or
INTELLIGENCE SUMMARY
CONFIDENTIAL.

(Erase heading not required.)

Instructions regarding War Diaries and Intelligence Summaries are contained in F. S. Regs, Part II. and the Staff Manual respectively. Title pages will be prepared in manuscript.

Place	Date	Hour	Summary of Events and Information	Remarks and references to Appendices
FORCEVILLE. P.27.b.1.2.	3/8/18.		Col.Clark. A.M.G.O. visited H.Q. and later went up the line with Major Kinsey. Capt. H.E.Smith, "A" Coy } Capt.H.G.P.McIlroy, "D" } Left for Course at G.H.Q., M.G.School. 1. O. R. "D" Company, rejoined ex Divisional Wing.	
FORCEVILLE. P.27.b.1.2.	4/8/18.		Officers Commanding Coys. 38th Battalion, M.G.C visited our O's.C.Coys, in the line to arrange details of relief. The third party of American troops completed their two days, period of individual training, and one complete American M.G.Coy (514th M.G.Bn) went into the line with "C" Coy for two day's instruction as a unit. 1.O.R. "A" Coy, 2.O.R. "D" Coy, proceeded on Leave to U.K.	
FORCEVILLE. P.27.b.1.2.	5/8/18.		During the night "D" Company was relieved by "C" Coy, 38th Bn.M.G.C. and proceeded on relief to the BROWN LINE, V.2.d. area adjoining HEDAUVILLE-WARLOi Road. "A" Coy were relieved by "D" Coy, 38th Bn M.G.C. and proceeded on relief to CORPS M.G.SCHOOL CAMP at T.5.a. (Near HERISSART) 15 O.R. "D" Coy, joined Battalion as reinforcements ex 21st M.G.Bn, (now at ACHEUX) 1.O.R. "D" Coy, proceeded on leave to U.K. On this date the first Armourer Sergt, ex Army Ordnance Corps recently added to the establishment, joined the Battalion.	
FORCEVILLE. P.27.b.1.2. & HERISSART. T.5.a.	6/8/18.		Battalion Headquarters closed at FORCEVILLE, P.27.b.1.2. at 3.p.m. and opened at CORPS M.G.SCHOOL, HERISSART, T.5.a. at the same time, Major Kinsey remaining at FORCEVILLE until relief of "B" & "C" Coys was reported complete. "B" & "C" Coys were relieved during the night by "A" & "B" Coys 38th Bn.M.G.C. respectively, proceeding on relief to join H.Q. & "A" Coy at Camp T.5.a. 1.O.R. "D" Coy, proceeded on leave to U.K.	
HERISSART. T.5.a.	7/8/18.		On completion of relief, the 17th Division becomes Right Supporting Division, V Corps, and in G.H.Q.Reserve, ready to move at 24 hours notice. The day was spent by Companies cleaning up and packing limbers. In the event of a move the Battalion will be attached as follows:- "A" Coy, to 50th Inf. Bde "B" Coy to 51st Inf. Bde.	

Army Form C. 2118.

WAR DIARY
or
INTELLIGENCE SUMMARY.   CONFIDENTIAL.

(Erase heading not required.)

Instructions regarding War Diaries and Intelligence Summaries are contained in F.S. Regs., Part II. and the Staff Manual respectively. Title pages will be prepared in manuscript.

Place	Date	Hour	Summary of Events and Information	Remarks and references to Appendices
HERISSART T.5.a.	8/8/18.		During the morning orders were received that the Battalion must be prepared to move at 2 hour's notice, the Division being in G.H.Q. reserve, and at 2.15 p.m. orders were received for a move to VECQUEMONT Area. "A" Coy moved with the 50th Inf. Bde.Group to BOIS L'ABBE, West of VILLERS-BRETONNEUX; "B" Coy with 51st Inf. Bde.Group to DAOURS; "C" & "D" & Battn.H.Q. with 52nd Inf. Bde. Group to BUSSY, arriving at 2.0.a.m. on the 9th. Route taken - TOUTENCOURT, CONTAY, BEAUCOURT, BEHENCOURT, FRECHENCOURT, PONT NOYELLES & QUERRIEU. The night was spent in billets. 1.O.R. "A" Coy & 1.O.R. "B" Coy proceeded on leave to U.K.	
BUSSY Sheet 62d 1/40,000.				
BUSSY. HEILLY.	9/8/18.		Morning and afternoon were spent resting, moves being ordered at 7.10.p.m. as follows:- "A" Coy with 50th Bde.Group to CORBIE, "B" Coy with 51st Bde.Group to vicinity of VAUX-SUR-SOMME, "C" & "D" Coys & Battn.H.Q. with 52nd Bde.Group to HEILLY, arriving at midnight. The night was spent in the open, the houses being unfit for occupation. Route taken by 52nd Bde.Group, - DAOURS, LA NEUVILLE, BONNAY.	
HEILLY.	10/8/18.		The whole day was spent resting at HEILLY.	
HEILLY. MORCOURT Q.16.a.4.4. Sheet 62d 1/40,000 & 62.d.SE. 1/20,000.	11/8/18.		Orders were received at 12 noon that the 17th Division will relieve the 3rd Australian Division in the Line immediately South of the SOMME, tonight. Lt-Col.D.B.Calder met G.S.O.1. 3rd Australian Division at P.7.c.1.8. to arrange details. "A" Coy moved from CORBIE to Right Sector with 50th Inf.Bde.Group via HAMELET staging in BOIS D'ACCROCHES Valley until dusk, when they relieved 9th Australian M.G.Coy. "B" Coy moved from VAUX-SUR-SOMME to the Left Sector with 51st Inf. Bde.Group via SAILLY-LE-SEC, SAILLY LAURETTE, staging at Assembly point West of CHERISY until dusk, when they relieved 11th Aust.M.G.Coy. "C" & "D" Coys moved by bus with 52nd Inf. Bde. Group to a point near HAMEL. "C" Coy then proceeded 23rd Aust.M.G.Coy near MORCOURT in Div.Reserve, with 52nd Brigade; "D" Coy relieved 23rd Aust.M.G.Coy in the GREEN LINE. Adv.Battn.H.Q. was established at MORCOURT, Q.16.a.4.4. Rear Battalion moved from HEILLY to VAUX-SUR-SOMME by Road, occupying camp vacated by "B" Coy, at J.26.d.8.8. Major R.G.Kinsey proceeded on leave to U.K.	

A 834   Wt.W4973/M687   750,000   8/16   D.D.&L.Ltd.   Forms/C.2118/13

WAR DIARY
or
INTELLIGENCE SUMMARY

CONFIDENTIAL.

Army Form C. 2118.

(Erase heading not required.)

Place	Date	Hour	Summary of Events and Information	Remarks and references to Appendices
MORCOURT. Q.16.a.4.4.	12/8/18.		Location of Coy. H.Q. are now as follows:- "A" Coy:- R.25.a.2.9. (Transport.Q.9.d.6.3.) "B" " Q.16.d.6.5. (.........Q.8.a.6.5.) "C" " Q.20.b.(REGINALD WOOD)(Transport Q.20.b.4.6.-"A" Echelon) (.........P.17.c.5.9.-"B" Echelon) "D" " Q.16.a.5.5. (Transport.J.26.d.8.8.with Rear Bn. H.Q.) O.C. "C" Coy reconnoitred positions in area Q.12.-Q.19 in compliance with Divisional Defence Scheme. 2/Lieut.A.K.Kingsmill, "C" Coy struck off strength on proceeding to Canada on leave. 2/Lieut.H.G.Rowles, "B" Coy, rejoined ex Veterinary Course.	
MORCOURT. Q.16.a.4.4.	13/8/18.		Rear Battalion H.Q. moved from VAUX to neighbourhood of HAMEL, P.9.a.3.3. accompanied by "D" Coy Transport. "C" Coy took up their new positions East of MORCOURT in conjunction with 52nd Inf.Bde. establishing Coy H.Q. at Q.18.a.20.25. O.C. "D" Coy reconnoitred positions for Defence of BROWN LINE in compliance with Divisional Defence Scheme. 3 O.R. "H".Q.;2.O.R."A" Coy; 2.O.R."B" Coy, proceeded to U.K. on leave. 2.O.R. "B" Coy, wounded and remained at duty, 2.O.R. "B" Coy wounded, 3.O.R. "B" Coy, wounded, - gas.	
MORCOURT. Q.16.a.4.4.	14/8/18.		"D" Coy took up new positions for the Defence of the BROWN LINE. During the night a heavy gas concentration was made by the enemy on R.l.d. area in which No.4.Section of "D" Coy was digging new emplacements. Two gun teams were gassed as a result of the explosion of a small dump of German gas bombs, caused by a direct-hit from a gas shell, and several others as the result of a gas shell bursting at the entrance of the bivouac in which they were sheltering. The remaining casualties were due to the action of the sun on the gas-drenched ground during the early morning of the 15th.inst. 1.O.R. "A" Coy. proceeded to U.K.- applicant for Commission. 1.O.R. "B" Coy killed in action, 1.O.R. "A" Coy wounded. Lieut.J.H.Underwood, "D" Coy, wounded, gas.	

Army Form C. 2118.

WAR DIARY
or
INTELLIGENCE SUMMARY
CONFIDENTIAL.

(Erase heading not required.)

Instructions regarding War Diaries and Intelligence Summaries are contained in F.S. Regs., Part II. and the Staff Manual respectively. Title pages will be prepared in manuscript.

Place	Date	Hour	Summary of Events and Information	Remarks and references to Appendices
MORCOURT. Q.16.a.4.4.	15/8/18.		Forward positions were taken up by "B" Coy under orders of G.O.C. 51st Inf. Bde. Lt.Col Marsden, D.S.O. Commanding 5th Australian M.G.Battalion visited forward Battalion H.Q. to arrange preliminary details of relief on the following day. Orders for relief were received from D.H.Q. at 8.45.p.m. 1.O.R. "D" Coy wounded. 2/Lieut.T.W.Quarmby, "D" Coy, struck off strength - previously accidentally injured.	
MORCOURT. Q.16.a.4.4. VECQUEMONT.	16/8/18.		Ordinary indirect fire, - 6250 rounds. "A" & "B" Coys were relieved by the 14th and 15th Coys of the 5th Australian M.G.Bn under Brigade arrangements, proceeding on relief to AUBIGNY & FOUILLOY respectively. "C" & "D" Coys were relieved by the 8th & 25th Coys of the 5th Australian M.G.Bn. and proceeded on relief to VECQUEMONT. Battalion H.Q.(Forward) closed at MORCOURT at 2.30.p.m. re-opening at VECQUEMONT at the same hour. Battalion H.Q. (rear) moved from HAMEL,P.9.a.3.3. to VECQUEMONT. 1.O.R. "A" Coy wounded. Lieut.A.W.Higgins, "B" Coy proceeded on leave to U.K.	
VECQUEMONT.	17/8/18.		Orders were received at 1.p.m. ex the 52nd Inf. Bde that "C" & "D" Coys, and Bn.H.Q. would move with 52nd Brigade Group to HERISSART, the Division transferring from the Australian Corps, Fourth Army, to V Corps. Lieut-Colonel W.A.Grierson, D.S.O. assumed Command of this Battalion, vice Lieut-Col.D.B.Calder. Battalion moved off at 9.35.p.m. followed by C.& D.Coys, Route taken - PONT NOYELLES & BEHENCOURT.	
HERISSART. Smith St Camp. Corps M.G.School. T.5.a.	18/8/18.		Camp was reached at 2.45 am. and "C" & "D" Coys were accommodated close to Battn.H.Q. During the forenoon, "Bn.H.Q." & "C" & "D" Coys moved across to the Camp vacated by the Battalion on the 8th inst. "A" Coy moved from AUBIGNY by Road with 50th Inf. Bde. Group, and "B" Coy from FOUILLOY with 51st Inf.Bde.Group, arriving in camp during the early morning of the 19th inst.	

Army Form C. 2118.

WAR DIARY
or
INTELLIGENCE SUMMARY. CONFIDENTIAL.

(Erase heading not required.)

Instructions regarding War Diaries and Intelligence Summaries are contained in F.S. Regs., Part II. and the Staff Manual respectively. Title pages will be prepared in manuscript.

Place	Date	Hour	Summary of Events and Information	Remarks and references to Appendices
HERISSART. CORPS M.G. SCHOOL.T.5.a.	19/8/18.		The day was spent making Camp improvements. Instructions received ex 17th Division at 4.30.p.m. to arrange for one company to join 38th Div at VARENNES on night 19th/20th and one company to be prepared to join 21st Div on 20th. for temporary duty. "C" Coy moved off at 9.0.p.m. to join 38th Div at VARENNES, establishing Coy.H.Q. in that village. Lt.F.H.Arnold, H.Q., proceeded on leave to U.K. 2/Lieuts.E.C.Filby, and H.Wade joined the Battalion as reinforcements and were posted to "A" Company. 17 O.R. joined the Battalion as reinforcements ex Div.Wing.	
HERISSART. Corps M.G. School. T.5.a.	20/8/18.		"D" Company moved off at 2.0.p.m. to join 21st Div at ACHEUX, subsequently taking up positions for firing barrage East of AUCHONVILLERS in which village Coy H.Q. were established in accordance with orders received at 12 noon ex 17th Div. "A" Coy proceeded to LEALVILLERS at 10.30.p.m. with 50th Inf. Bde.Group. "C" Coy moved from VARENNES. 2/Lt.H.G.Maschwitz, and 2/Lt K.J.Epsworth joined the Battalion as Reinforcements and were posted to C.&.D.Coys. respectively. 40 O.R. joined the battalion as reinforcements ex Div.Wing. 1.O.R. "A" Coy proceeded on leave to U.K. 1.O.R. "D" Coy, proceeded to U.K. Candidate for Commission. 2/Lt.H.A.Disney M.C. proceeded on leave to U.K.	
HERISSART Corps M.G. School.T.5.a.	21/8/18.	dawn.	Barrages were fired by C.&.D.Companies in support of an attack by the 21st Div.at dawn. At dusk "C" & "D" Coys took up positions covering ENGELBELMER and MAILLET-MAILLY respectively under orders of 21st. M.G.Bn establishing Coy.H.Q. at P.24.d.3.4. and P.5.d.3.1. Orders were received from 17th Div. at 10.30.p.m. that "C" & "D" Coys would return forthwith to 17th Div, and in accordance with instructions "C" Coy was then placed at the tactical disposal of the 52nd Infantry Brigade and ordered by the latter to concentrate in the neighbourhood of its present Coy H.Q. being transferred to P.6.d.15.70. "A" Coy moved from LEALVILLERS to ENGELBELMER with 50th Bde Group and established H.Q. at Q.20.a.25.05. "B" Coy moved to LEALVILLERS at 1.45 p.m. with 51st Inf.Bde Group, thence to P.27.d.7.7. between HEDAUVILLE & FORCEVILLE where Coy H.Q. were established. From 8.0.a.m. 21st, the 17th Div is at ½ hrs notice.	

Army Form C. 2118.

WAR DIARY
or
INTELLIGENCE SUMMARY

CONFIDENTIAL.

(Erase heading not required.)

Instructions regarding War Diaries and Intelligence
Summaries are contained in F. S. Regs., Part II
and the Staff Manual respectively. Title pages
will be prepared in manuscript.

Place	Date	Hour	Summary of Events and Information	Remarks and references to Appendices
HERISSART. Corps M.G. School.T.5.a.	22/8/18.		"B" "C" & "D" Coys did not move. "A" Coy with 50th Inf.Bde. relieved the front held by 110th Inf.Bde. 21st Div during the night. Brigade boundaries as follows:- Northern, R.14.c.0.0. to Q.12.c.6.0. thence West along Grid 14nd between Q.11. & Q.17. Southern, THIEPVAL ROAD (Exclusive) C.O. attended Conference at Div.H.Q. at 6.30.p.m. (TOUTENCOURT) Major P.G.Fry, (O.C.) 2/Lt Etheridge and I.O."D" Coy wounded by bombs. 2/Lt Leetch instructed to Command "D" Coy until further orders. Capt. & Rev.T.S.Rogerson, Chaplain, proceeded on 14 O.R.proceeded on leave to U.K. leave to U.K. W/Capt.J.S.Walker assumed Command of "D" Coy, vice A/Major P.G.Fry.	
HERISSART. Corps M.G. School.T.5.a.	23/8/18.		C.O. met Coy Commanders of "B","C" & "D" Coys to reconnoitre for suitable battery positions from which to support an attack by 50th Brigade, and Brigades of 21st Div and 38th Div on Left and Right Flanks respectively. "A" Coy to go forward with 50th Brigade in the attack. At 11.0.a.m. C.O. was present at Conference at 50th Brigade H.Q. at Q.9.c.6.5. to arrange details of attack. 1 Section with West Yorks, 1 with East Yorks, and 2 with Dorsets. Owing to alteration of Infantry Starting point, barrages to be fired by "B" "C" & "D" Coys were cancelled. "B" Coy had one gun which fell off a runaway mule run over by a limber, and another gun lost by falling into the ANCRE whilst crossing. "B" Coy crossed the ANCRE after dusk, establishing Coy H.Q. at Q.17.central. "A" Coy's H.Q. after relief of 110th Inf.Bde. were at Q.18.d.8.8. "C" & "D" Coys remained concentrated in the neighbourhood of AUCHONVILLERS. ("C" Coy H.Q. - Q.3.d.9.2. "D" Coys H.Q. - Q.9.a.8.2.) C.O. remained with 50th Inf.Bde. whose H.Q. removed to Q.17.c.9.9. prior to the attack at 1.0.a.m. 24th inst. 17 O.R. joined the Battalion as reinforcements ex Div Wing. 8 O.R. previously evacuated through sickness and wounds, rejoined ex Div Wing.	
HERISSART Corps M.G. School.T.5.a.	24/8/18.		After the attack the C.O. moved forward to R.26.a.5.8. with 50th and 52nd Inf. Bdes, and H.Q. of "A" & "B" Coys were also transferred to there. "C" Coy moved forward to join 52nd Bde Group, establishing H.Q. at the same point. "D" Coy moved forward after dark from AUCHONVILLERS to occupy reserve positions in R.25.a.&.c. Battalion Headquarters moved to No.23. billet BEAUSSART, leaving HERISSART at 7.15.a.m.	

Army Form C. 2118.

WAR DIARY
or
INTELLIGENCE SUMMARY.
CONFIDENTIAL.

(Erase heading not required.)

Instructions regarding War Diaries and Intelligence Summaries are contained in F. S. Regs., Part II. and the Staff Manual respectively. Title pages will be prepared in manuscript.

Place	Date	Hour	Summary of Events and Information	Remarks and references to Appendices
BEAUSSART. Billet 23. Q.17.c.7.3. Sheet 57D.SE	25/8/18.		In order to facilitate communications between Coy H.Q. and Batt.H.Q. a Runner Relay Post was established at Mouquet Farm R.33.b.6.8. "D" Coy became attached to 50th Bde at R.26.a.5.8. Advance was continued by 52nd Brigade at 4.0.a.m. with "C" Coy, one Section accompanying 10th Lanc. Fus, on Left, one Section 12th Manchesters on Right, remaining two sections were held in Brigade Reserve, and advanced in rear of 9th Dule of Wellingtons. All sections advanced using Pack, taking 8 belt boxes per gun. Two forward sections eventually reached Sunken Road at S.2.a.40.95. (Sheet 57C.SW.) Right of MARTINPUICH, the left section having been transferred to this point as little opposition had been encountered on the left, and the right flank was considered dangerous. These two sections were unable to move from the Sunken Road owing to heavy M.G. Fire from HIGH WOOD. They had already suffered five casualties and had a gun and one mule put out of action also. Shortly afterwards 2/Lt E.G. Mungeam was seriously wounded and died before he could be got to the Dressing Station. Reserve Sections halted at the SUGAR REFINERY, COURCELETTE and Coy H.Q. moved forward to R.35.d.5.8. at 9.30.a.m. with H.Q.52nd Brigade. Later it was decided to continue the advance of the 10th Lancs.Fus. and the left Companies of the 12th Manchester Regt, and 6 guns from the teams in reserve were sent to support them, the two sections in the Sunken Rd automatically becoming Brigade reserve. These guns had been used during the morning to neutralise enemy M.G. in HIGH WOOD in support of the advances of the Infantry. At 7.30.p.m. the six guns referred to above were disposed as follows :- 4 just East, and 2 just West of MARTINPUICH with, 2/Lt Looms in charge. 2/Lt T.Halstead, who also accompanied these guns when they were sent forward from the SUGAR REFINERY, was wounded by shell fire shortly after arrival in position. H.Q. "A" & "B" Coys moved forward to neighbourhood of SUGAR REFINERY, COURCELETTE, and "D" Coy to M.26.b.5.3.with Bde Group. During the day the "B" Echelons of all companies were concentrated at Q.17.c.7.3. (Near HAMEL) with Battalion H.Q., the latter having moved forward from BEAUSSART at 1.15.p.m. It was arranged that, in future "B" Echelons of all companies would remain with Battalion H.Q. irrespective of whether Companies were attached to Brigades or not. 2/Lt.K.J.Ebsworth, "D" Coy, wounded in action, 1.O.R. "A" Coy, Killed in action. 1.O.R. "A" Coy, 2 O.R. "B"Coy, 5 O.R. "C" Coy Wounded. 1.O.R. "C" Coy Killed in action.	

WAR DIARY
or
INTELLIGENCE SUMMARY.

Army Form C. 2118.
CONFIDENTIAL.

(Erase heading not required.)

Place	Date	Hour	Summary of Events and Information	Remarks and references to Appendices
Q.17.c.7.3. Sheet 57D.SE.	26/8/18.		An advance was made at 5.0.am. with 52nd Bde on Right, supported by "C" Coy and 51st Bde on Left supported by "B" Coy, 50th Bde following 52nd Bde with "A" Coy. "D" Coy remained in Reserve. "C" Coy increased the six teams in vicinity of MARTINPUICH to 8, and they followed Infantry to neighbourhood of Cross Roads M.35.d.9.9. on the left and squares S.5.a.& b. on the right. Four teams from Brigade reserve at the SUGAR REFINERY were sent to vicinity of SEVEN ELMS, M.28.d. During this advance another mule was wounded in the leg. Guns of "B" Coy had taken up general line prior to the advance as follows:- M.17.central, - M.23.central, -M.28.a.2.0. and in addition to pack mules for guns tripods etc, each section had four mules on which to carry ammunition. The left flank section (accompanying Border Regt) aided the infantry with direct overhead fire on to the Ridge running SE of MARTINPUICH - WARLENCOURT ROAD and casualties were seen to be incurred by the enemy. "A" Company had one gun put out of action. 1 O.R. "D" Coy wounded, Capt. C.G.Schurr detached to Field Ambulance Advanced Dressing Station.	
Q.17.c.7.3. GRAVEL PIT at R.34.a.0.4. Sheet 57D.SE.	27/8/18.		Objectives for this day's operations was Ridge running North and South through N.28. 50th Brigade with "A" & "D" Companies passed through 52nd and 51st Brigades and commenced the attack at 1.0.a.m. Guns of "A" Coy advanced through village of FLERS with Infantry but were forced to retire with them, and subsequently took up positions as follows:- 1 section 3 guns in Front line from N.19.c.5.0. to N.23.a.3.1. 2 sections about M.29.d. and the remaining section protecting right flank of West Yorks Regt. Guns of "D" Coy were detailed to protect the flanks of the Bde and two sections took up positions in depth on either flank. "A" Coy H.Q. moved forward close to SEVEN ELMS in the evening, also "D" Coy H.Q. 50th Brigade H.Q., have moved forward to SEVEN ELMS, at 3.30.p.m. "B" Coys guns took up supporting positions from M.24.central to M.29.d.central, and Coy H.Q. moved forward to M.28.a.3.3. "C" Coys guns were withdrawn into reserve with 52nd Brigade and concentrated in MARTINPUICH, Coy H.Q. being established in the village. Battalion H.Q. Moved forward to GRAVEL PIT at R.34.a.0.4.(Sheet 57D.SE) Runner Relay Post moved forward from MOUQUET FARM R.33.b.6.3. to SUGAR REFINERY, COURCELETTE.	

Army Form C. 2118.

WAR DIARY
or
INTELLIGENCE SUMMARY. CONFIDENTIAL.
(Erase heading not required.)

Instructions regarding War Diaries and Intelligence Summaries are contained in F. S. Regs., Part II. and the Staff Manual respectively. Title pages will be prepared in manuscript.

Place	Date	Hour	Summary of Events and Information	Remarks and references to Appendices
GRAVEL PIT. R.34.a.0.4. Sheet 57D.SE.	27/8/18.		During the afternoon Major D.Haugh.M.C. Commanding "B" Coy, was wounded. Weather became showery during the afternoon. 2/Lt.G.T.Fraser assumed Command of "B" Coy. 3.O.R. "A" Coy wounded, 7.O.R. "C" Coy wounded, 6.O.R. "D" Coy. wounded, 2/Lt.S.Leetch "D" Coy, wounded, remained at duty. Relay Post established at SUGAR REFINERY COURCELETTE. 2/Lt.F.Perch "A" Coy to be Lieutenant from 1/4/18, Auth'y.London Gazette 27/5/18.	
GRAVEL PIT R.34.A.0.4. Sheet. 57D.SE	28/8/18.		No advance has been ordered for today, as the Right Division has not been able to advance forward. Relay Post established at M.33.a.1.8. 3.O.R."A" Coy. Killed in action; 1.O.R. "D" Coy. Killed in action; 6 O.R. "A" Coy, wounded; 3 O.R. "B" Coy, wounded; "D" Coy, wounded. 2/Lt.E.G.Fibb "A" Coy, wounded in action; 2/Lt.S.Leetch "D" Coy evacuated wounded. No.43929.Pte.Leonard H.H. "B" Coy awarded Bounty of £15 under A.O. 209/1916. No.14812.Sgt.Munn.A.J. "B" Coy, awarded Meritorious Service Medal, Auth'y, London Gazette dated 17/6/18.	
GRAVEL PIT. R.34.A.0.4. Sheet 57D.SE	29/8/18.		"C" Coy relieved "A" Coy and came under the Tactical control of 51 Bde; "C" & "D" Coys. came under the Tactical control of 51 Bde. "B" Coy under 52 Bde; "B" & "D" Coys. (32 guns) put down a barrage from the right of MARTINPUICH to assist 38th Division in their attack on the high ground East of GINCHY. After the barrage the Companies came under the tactical control of the Brigades as stated above. At 10.p.m. the Division moved forward, with the exception of the Reserve Bde, and "A" Coy to positions as follows:- 51 Bde on the line in front of GUEUDECOURT and FLERS. "C" Coys guns covered left and "D" Coy Right flanks, echeloned in depth 52 Bde in support with "B" Coy. 50th Bde in reserve. "D" Coy H.Q. N.27.c.5.9. "C" Coy N.27.c.2.7. "B" Coy.M.29.c.3.3. "A" Coy.M.33.a.1.9. Relay Post established at N.29.c.8.3. Lt.&.Q.M. J.T.Bill granted leave to U.K. from 29/8/18 to 12/9/18. 7.O.R. granted leave to U.K. from 1/9/18, to 15/9/18.	

Army Form C. 2118.

WAR DIARY
or
INTELLIGENCE SUMMARY. CONFIDENTIAL.
(Erase heading not required.)

Instructions regarding War Diaries and Intelligence
Summaries are contained in F.S. Regs., Part II
and the Staff Manual respectively. Title pages
will be prepared in manuscript.

Place	Date	Hour	Summary of Events and Information	Remarks and references to Appendices
Sheet 57D.SE. R.34.a.0.4. M.28.d.3.0. Sheet 57C.SW.	30/8/18.		Battalion H.Q. moved forward at 8.0.a.m. to M.28.d.3.0. 52nd Bde relieved 51st Brigade during night 30/31st August, as advanced guard brigade. "B" Coy relieved "D" Coy. "C" & "B" Coys came under tactical control of G.O.C. 52 Bde. 50 Bde relieved 52 Bde as supporting brigade. "A" Coy relieved "B" Coy in supports, and came under tactical control of G.O.C. 50th Bde. 51 Bde became Bde in Div Reserve. "D" Coy moved back in reserve to position near Battalion H.Q. and came under Tactical control of G.O.C. 51 Bde. The guns of "B" & "C" Coys were echeloned in depth on flanks of 52 Bde in front of GUEUDECOURT. The guns of "A" Coys were concentrated in support behind GUEUDECOURT. Relay post established at M.19.d.3.1. Lt.W.P.Allen, M.C. assumed Command of "D" Coy, vice A/Capt.J.S.Walker, admitted to hospital sick. 2/Lt.I.C.Jenkins rejoined the Battalion as reinforcement, and was posted to "B" Coy. 6.O.R. rejoined from leave to U.K. 1.O.R. "C" Coy wounded.	
M.28.d.3.0. Sheet 57C.SW.	31/8/18.		No advance was made today. Orders were received at 11.p.m. that the Division in conjunction with 21st Div on left and 38th Div on right would carry out an attack on the morning of the 1st, preliminary operations being 52 Bde to attack and gain line N.35.d.3.a. -line of road to N.35.b.2.9. thence Sunken Road to N.30.c.1.5. thence line of Trench Northwards to N.29.b. about midnight 31st/1st. Main operation. 52 Bde to attack front in N.23.c. objective trenches East of BAPAUME - PERONNE ROAD - N.24.d. and 0.19.c. 50 Bde to be responsible for the defence in case of counter attack of Ridge N.35.c.- N.22.central M.G.Barrage to fire on the BAPAUME - PERONNE ROAD and SUGAR FACTORY. 8 guns "C" Coy at N.28.a. and 8 guns "B" Coy at N.34.a. were detailed. Owing however to the rapid rate of advance of the troops and the preliminary attack to gain ground, the barrage could only last for eight minutes. "A" Coy was attached to 50 Bde, and responsible for the defence of the area in case of counter attack. "D" Coy was in reserve awaiting orders from 51 Bde to move forward to Ridge between FLERS & GUEUDECOURT. 2/Lt.C.J.Devey promoted Lieutenant from 19/7/18. 2/Lt.G.T.Fraser promoted Lieutenant from 26/7/18. Authority London Gazette dated 31/8/18. A/Capt.J.S.Walker evacuated sick out of Corps Area 30/8/18.	

Strength of Battalion....37 Officers.   808 Other Ranks.

SECRET.

COPY No. 4

17th Battalion, Machine Gun Corps, Order No.28.

In the Field.
20-8-18.

1. "A" Company will move in accordance with 50th Infantry Brigade Order No.230.

2. All Packs and Greatcoats will be dumped at the Battalion Quartermaster's Stores by 9.0.p.m. tonight.

3. A Nominal Roll of Battle Surplus will be given to the Adjutant before moving off. Battle surplus will remain at this Camp.

4. Trench Strengths will be sent in to Battalion Headquarters every morning as usual.

Capt. & Adjt.,
17th Battalion, M.G.C.

Copies to:-

No.1. "A" Company.
2. File.
3. Quartermaster.

Army Form C. 2118.

WAR DIARY
or
INTELLIGENCE SUMMARY.
(Erase heading not required.)

Confidential.

WAR DIARY

OF

17th Battalion M G Corps

From 1.ix.18 to 30.ix.18

WAR DIARY
or
INTELLIGENCE SUMMARY

CONFIDENTIAL.

Army Form C. 2118.

Place	Date	Hour	Summary of Events and Information	Remarks and references to Appendices
Sheet 57C. M.28.d.3.0.	1/9/18.		SEPTEMBER 1918. STRENGTH OF BATTALION --- 37 Officers, 803 Other Ranks. The attack as ordered last night, took place at 5.40.a.m. but owing to heavy machine gun fire from the direction of LE TRANSLOI CEMETERY, the Infantry were unable to gain their objective. One section of "C" Company was detailed to Support Battalion, one section to Reserve Battalion, and two sections on high ground between GUEUDECOURT & LE TRANSLOI occupied defensive positions for the remainder of the day. "A" Company moved its Headquarters to N.27.b.5.2. at 5.0.a.m. 50th Bde established its Headquarters at the H.Q. of 52nd Bde. Enemy Machine Guns and snipers were active during the day. 21st Divn on Left took BEAULENCOURT, - 38th Divn on Right took MORVAL. At 10.0p.m. orders were received that 52nd Bde would attack from the line of the Road T.6.a.5.0. - T.5.b.0.7. 1st Objective, - BAPAUME PERONNE Road; 2nd Objective RIDGE 0.32.b.7.5. - 0.25.d.7.6. The 21st Divn on Left to attack SUGAR FACTORY and to push on to 0.19.d.central at 2.0.am. and at 5.0.a.m. to capture LUBDA COPSE and SPUR in 0.13.d. The attacks of the 17th Divn. to commence at 5.0.a.m. 2nd Septr. and to be carried out on a frontage of two Battalions, with one Battalion in Support. When final objectives were gained, two Companies were to be pushed forward Northwards to 0.19.d.central to gain touch with 21st Divn. and block egress Eastwards of enemy from LE TRANSLOY. All available guns of "A" & "C" Coys were detailed to fire a barrage within safety limits on the left flank of the attack, as far North as LES BOEUFS Road-CHURCH Street between 5.0.a.m. and 6.30.a.m. "B" Company was placed at the disposal of G.O.C. 52nd Bde, to accompany the attack. 51st. Bde were to move forward at 6.30.am to neighbourhood of FLERS-GUEUDECOURT. "D" Coy to take orders to move from 51st Bde. Captain F.J.A.Dibdin MC, and 2/Lieut.H.Roberts joined Battalion as reinforcements from Base Depot, and were posted to "D" Company. Captain F.M.Thomas joined Battalion as reinforcement from Base Depot, and posted to Headquarters. Capt. F.J.A.Dibdin MC assumed Command of "D" Company from Lieut.W.P.Allen.MC. Lieut.G.S.M.Morgen. "A" Company, Wounded in action 1/9/18. 2-O.R. "A" Coy wounded; 4-O.R. "B" Coy wounded, 1 -O.R. "C" Coy wounded. W.O.R. joined from leave to U.K. and 12 A.S.R with O.R. Nos. 4973165, Bat. 66-18/40nd 98 & Reinforcements, from Base Depot.	

WAR DIARY or **INTELLIGENCE SUMMARY**

Army Form C. 2118.
CONFIDENTIAL.

Place	Date	Hour	Summary of Events and Information	Remarks and references to Appendices
MARTINPUICH M.28.d.3.0.	2/9/18.		Report timed 7.30.a.m. states that leading troops have crossed the BAPAUME-PERONNE Road and advancing on 1st objective with slight opposition and few casualties. 6 guns "C" Coy fired a barrage on LE TRANSLOY. 18000 rdss being fired in support of the attack. 4 guns "A" Coy fired a barrage on LE TRANSLOY, 6000 rds being fired. Orders were received that 52nd Bde should resume the attack at 5.10 p.m. to gain line 0.33.c.0.4. - 0.26.d.0.0. - 0.14.a.3.0. objective ROCQUIGNY(Inclusive) and line of Road 0.27.b.5.2. - 0.21.d.5.7. "A" & "C" Coys were placed at the disposal of G.O.C. 50 Bde; "D" Coy at the disposal of 51 Bde, to be prepared to move to Line N.35.-N.22 and to move forward at short notice. "B" Coy was placed at the disposal of 52 Bde which would come into reserve. "D" Company moved H.Q. to N.21.b.2.1. ROCQUIGNY was captured during the night and 27 prisoners taken. 21st Div. came out into Corps Reserve under junction of the 17th and 42nd Div on left. A/Major R.G Kinsey.MC. "H.Q" Granted extension of leave to 3/9/18.	
MARTINPUICH M.28.d.3.0. N.23.a.2.1.	3/9/18.		At 8.0.a.m. Enemy reported holding iTRES-ETRICOURT line. "A" Coy moved H.Q. to 0.21.c.0.0. "D" Coy moved H.Q. to N.24.c.1.2. "C" Coy moved H.Q. to N.27.b.0.2. Battalion H.Q. moved at noon to N.23.a.2.1. During the afternoon "A" Coy moved H.Q. to 0.30.c.0.0. "C" Coy moved H.Q. to 0.29.d.9.2. "D" Coy moved H.Q. to 0.22.c.3.4. "B" Coy moved H.Q. to 0.23.c.0.7. Relay Post established at M.27.a.7.6. 4.0.R "D" Coy wounded.	
BEAULENCOURT N.23.a.3.0	4/9/18.		Line advanced over CANAL DU NORD at 6.0.a.m. No change in Coy Headquarters. Casualties 1.O.R.	
BEAULENCOURT N.23.a.3.0.	5/9/18.		"D" Coy relieved "C" Coy in the Advance Guard positions. "A" & "D" Coys then came under the Tactical control of G.O.C. 51 Bde Advance Guard. "C" Coy with Support Bde (50th) "B" Coy with reserve Bde (52) H.Q's, "A" Coy P.31.c.90.50. "D" Coy P.31.c.6.6. "C" Coy 0.29.d.9.2. "B" Coy 0.23.c.0.7. 2/Lieut.R.Northcote joined Battalion as reinforcement from Base Depot and posted to "D" Coy. 28 O.R. joined as reinforcements. Casualties, 8.O.R.Wounded. 2/Lieut.R.A.Pleace, 2/Lieut.T.Rawlinson, 2/Lieut.H.G.Holoren, Capt.H.G.P.McIlroy returned from Courses. Lieut.A.W.Higgins rejoined from leave.	

Army Form C. 2118.

WAR DIARY
or
INTELLIGENCE SUMMARY

CONFIDENTIAL.

(Erase heading not required.)

Instructions regarding War Diaries and Intelligence Summaries are contained in F.S. Regs., Part II. and the Staff Manual respectively. Title pages will be prepared in manuscript.

Place	Date	Hour	Summary of Events and Information	Remarks and references to Appendices
BEAULENCOURT. N.23.a.3.0. LECHELLE WOOD O.36.d.5.9.	6/9/18.		"B" Coy relieved "A" Coy in Trench System in P.34 and V.4. "A" Coy moved to P.34.d.00.40. "B" & "D" Coys formed part of Advanced Guard Bde and came under the Tactical Control of G.O.C. 52nd Bde. Attack by Border Regt supported by covering fire. Many targets engaged. "C" Coy in reserve with 50th Bde in O.29.d. Batt H.Q. moved to O.36.d.5.9. near LECHELLE WOOD. 2/Lts.E.Newton, and A&R.R.J.Osbourn joined Battalion as reinforcements from Base Depot. 2.O.R. wounded in action, 3.O.R. gassed in action. Lieut.A.Abrahams transferred to 56th Div; A/Capt.H.G.P.McIlroy granted leave to U.K. Major R.G.Kinsey.MC. rejoined from Leave to U.K.	
LECHELLE WOOD. O.36.d.5.9.	7/9/18.		At 6.0.a.m. "B" & "D" Coys moved forward with Advanced Guard Bde and supported Infantry attacks Direct overhead fire employed from V.4.b. into DESSART WOOD. Locations:- "A" Coy,V.2.b.30.30; "B" Coy, V.5.b.5.3; "C" Coy, O.29.d. and "D" Coy V.5.b.5.3. 2 O.R. wounded in action.	
LECHELLE WOOD. O.36.d.5.9.	8/9/18.		"C" Coy relieved "D" Coy and came under the Tactical control of G.O.C. 50th Bde. "B" Coy came under the Tactical Control of G.O.C. 50th Bde. The dispositions of Coys were as follows:- "A" Company with 51st Bde in Support at V.2.b.20.30. "B" & "D" Coys with 50th Bde Advance Guard V.5.b.5.3. "C" Company with 52nd Bde in Reserve at FOUR WINDS FARM. 2/Lieuts.H.G.Head, and R.E.Trethewey joined Battalion as reinforcements from Base Depot and posted to Companies. 2.O.R. wounded in action, 3.O.R. Died of wounds.	
LECHELLE WOOD. O.36.d.5.9.	9/9/18.		Infantry attack on HEATHER SUPPORT TRENCH supported by barrage fire from "B" & "D" Coys. Harassing fire continued throughout the day by "B" Company. "D" Company followed the Infantry closely and consolidated, driving off repeated counterattacks. Infantry attacked; 1st objective HEATHER SUPPORT. 2nd objective HEATHER TRENCH. "B" Coy fired barrage from 4.20. to 4.35 on both flanks of the attack, and then moved forward, carrying out direct fire on AFRICAN TRENCH SUPPORT and harassing fire on roads. 2 sections of "D" Coy fired on HEATHER TRENCH and two followed infantry closely, and consolidated on HEATHER SUPPORT. HEATHER TRENCH not taken. Repeated enemy counter attacks on HEATHER SUPPORT were driven off. An attempt on the part of the enemy to outflank, was stopped by Lewis Guns, and one machine gun was captured from the enemy and used against them. Locations:- "A" - V.2.b.20.34.	

WAR DIARY
or
INTELLIGENCE SUMMARY

Army Form C. 2118. CONFIDENTIAL.

(Erase heading not required.)

Place	Date	Hour	Summary of Events and Information	Remarks and references to Appendices
LECHELLE WOOD. 0.36.d.5.9.	10/9/18.		"C" Company relieved "D" Company in the line. 3.O.R. Killed in action, 10.O.R. Wounded in action. 2/Lieut.T.Rawlinson, wounded remained at duty; 2.O.R. wounded remained at duty Lieut.F.H.Arnold and 2/Lieut.H.A.Disney.MC.DCM. rejoined from leave to U.K. Location "A" Company, - V.6.a.00.80.	
LECHELLE WOOD. 0.36.d.5.9.	11/9/18.		Division relieved in the line by the 38th Division. Battalion moved back to ROCQUIGNI. Lieut.F.H.Arnold appointed 2nd i/c "B" Company on returning from Leave to U.K. Military Medal awarded to 3.O.R. "D" Company, and 1.O.R. "B" Coy.	
ROCQUIGNY. 0.22.d.	12/9/18.		Battalion in rest. Inspections and general cleaning up. C.O's Conference held at 4.30.p.m. Congratulations received from Corps Commander on recent operations.	
ROCQUIGNY. 0.22.d.	13/9/18.		"D" Company bathed; "A" & "B" Coys inspected on Pack Drill by C.O. Capt. & Rev. T.S.Rogerson rejoined from leave to U.K.	
ROCQUIGNY. 0.22.d.	14/9/18.		Remainder of Battalion bathed. Voluntary Church Services held.	
ROCQUIGNY. 0.22.d.	15/9/18.		2/Lieuts. T.L.Smith, M.W.Penman, & T.H.Waddell joined Battalion as reinforcements from Base Depot. 69 O.R. joined Battalion as reinforcements from Base Depot. Lieut.& QM. J.T.Bill, rejoined from Leave to U.K.	
ROCQUIGNY. 0.22.d.	16/9/18.		In the evening, "A" Coy moved forward to 1.6.c.80.80. FTNS. 2/Lieut.J.W.Jones, and 30 O.R. joined Battalion as reinforcements from Base Depot.	
ROCQUIGNY. 0.22.d.	17/9/18.		Orders issued for an attack on the Corps front 17/18th on which "B" "& "D" Coys 33rd Battalion, M.G.C are assisting this Division with 32 guns for barrage purposes. The intention of this Division is to take the outskirts of the South end of GOUZEAUCOURT, and is to be made in three bounds. "A" Coy is attached to 50 Bdex "B" Coy to 51 Bde and accompany these attacking Bdes. "C" & "D" Coys, are, on the final objective being taken, to push forward their guns for protective S.O.S. Location of Company Headquarters are as follows tonight:- "A", "C" & "D" 17th M.G.Bn.-W.9.d.7.0.) "B" Coy,17th Bn.M.G.C. at "B", & "D" 33rd M.G.Bn....W.9.d.7.0.) 50th/52nd Bde Headquarters. W.9.a.central,-51 Bde H.Q. Rev. W.W.W.W.W.W.W.W.W.W.W.W.W.W.W.W.W.W.W.W. transferred to M.G.C. "C" Coy.	

WAR DIARY or **INTELLIGENCE SUMMARY**

Army Form C. 2118. CONFIDENTIAL.

Place	Date	Hour	Summary of Events and Information	Remarks and references to Appendices
LE MESNIL EN ARROUAISE. U.11.d.9.1.	18/9/18.		The attack as ordered took place at 5.20.a.m. The first objective was taken by the 52nd Infy Bde and comprised CHAPEL REDOUBT & CHAPEL TRENCH. 50th Inf Bde supported by "A" Company then went through and took up positions in the second objective which was RACKET TRENCH. 52nd Inf Bde supported by "B" Coy then passed through 50th Bde to final objective which was BEET TRENCH. Dispositions of "B" Coys guns at 6.30.p.m. were as follows:- 2 guns CHAPEL ALLEY X.7.a.5.6. firing N.E. 2 guns BEET TRENCH X.8.a.45.55. covering VILLERS GUISLAIN and VILLERS TRENCH, 2 guns X.8.a.60.25 firing from POPP⊥ POST To VILLERS GUISLAIN, 2 guns CHAPEL ALLEY X.7.a.85.60 firing N.E; 2 guns CHAPEL TRENCH X.7.b.00.65 firing N.W; 4 guns SUNKEN Rd W.6.d.65.20. covering GOUZEAUCOURT VALLEY and GAUCHE WOOD. Guns of "A" Coy were disposed to cover Left Flank S. of GOUZEAUCOURT situation on left flank being obscure owing to loss of touch with the 38th Division. "C" & "D" Coys were organised as Barrage batteries. "C" Coy fired from Z to Z plus 143 mins from positions N.E. of HEUDECOURT in W.4.d. and W.10.b. moving forward after final objective had been taken to positions on CHAPEL HILL from which S.O.S. barrage could be fired on Western outskirts of VILLERS GUISLAIN. "C" Coy Adv H.Q. were established at CHAPEL CROSSING X.7.6. "D" Coy fired for 14 mins to cover Infy advance on to area W.6.d. and then moved forward to X.5.c. to support the attack at 9.0.a.m. to U.11.d.9.1. and Rear Battalion Headquarters moved forward at 9.0.a.m. to U.11.d.9.1. and forward Battalion Headquarters were established at W.9.c.7.2. Locations of Coy H.Q. as follows:- "A" - W.9.d.7.0; "B" - X.7.c.00.70.; "C" - Rear H.Q. at W.15.b.10.80; Adv H.Q. as stated; "D" W.9.d.7.0. "C" Coy fired three times in response to the S.O.S.Signal, 90,000 rds fired. Casualties, 2 O.R. wounded, and 2/Lieut.R.A.Pleace admitted to hospital suffering from the effects of gas.	
LE MESNIL EN ARROUAISE. U.11.d.9.1.	19/9/18.		No.3.section "B" Coy withdrew from BEET TRENCH to FIVES Trench as the BORDERS had been bombed out of LANCASHIRE Trench and positions were taken up as follows:- 2 guns X.7.d.4.8. and 2 guns X.7.d.5.5. covering all approaches from VILLERS GUISLAIN. About 9.0.p.m. a re-adjustment of the Companies took place owing to the alterations in the Divisional Boundaries. "A" Coy then took up positions commencing the approaches to GOUZEAUCOURT. "B" Company guns were disposed as follows:- 3 guns SOMME ALLEY firing E. and N.E. four guns LOWLAND TRENCH firing N.E. Four guns QUENTIN REDOUBT 2 guns W.6.d.65.45. firing N, 2 guns W.6.d.95.35. firing N.E. "C" Coy moved back to the vicinity of their original barrage positions for the previous days attack, and S.O.S.lines laid out to cover the village N.&.S. of GOUZEAUCOURT. Immediately before moving, fire was opened in response to the S.O.S. Signal but no serious attack developed. "D" Coy batteries moved to Area W.12.c.&.d. covering VILLERS GUISLAIN and GOUZEAUCOURT.	

Army Form C. 2118.

WAR DIARY
or
INTELLIGENCE SUMMARY.   CONFIDENTIAL.
(Erase heading not required.)

Instructions regarding War Diaries and Intelligence Summaries are contained in F.S. Regs., Part II. and the Staff Manual respectively. Title pages will be prepared in manuscript.

COMMANDING 17 BATTN. M.G. CORPS.
LIEUT. COLONEL.

Place	Date	Hour	Summary of Events and Information	Remarks and references to Appendices
LE MESNIL EN ARROUAISE. U.11.d.9.1.	19/9/18.		Locations of Coy H.Q. "A" "C" & "D" .. W.9.d.7.2. "B" - W.12.d.9.1. Adv.Bn.H.Q. - No change. 5.O.R. Killed in action, 14 O.R. wounded. 2/Lieut.A.R.K.J.Osbourn admitted to hospital, gassed; 2/Lieut.H.Holland, evacuated sick.	
...do...	20/9/18.		Divisional Boundaries have been adjusted as follows :- Northern Boundary, GOUZEAUCOURT-FINS Rd to W.3.central- Southern Boundary, LANCASHIRE Trench -G AUCHE ALLEY to Sunken Road in W.12.b. thence to W.11 central. 51st and 52nd Bdes were relieved Southwards of the line LANCASHIRE SUPPORT GAUCHE ALLEY by 9th Bde, 33rd Division. 52nd Bde relieved 114th Bde 38th Division front as far North as RUE D'ENFER 50th Bde then extended South and took over as far as line held by 51st Bde, which came into Divisional reserve. Locations for Coy H.Q's same as for 19th, except "B" Coy whose H.Q. moved to CHAPEL HILL W.18.a.2.9. "C" Coy did harassing fire on enemy lines of approach from barrage positions. 25,000 rds being fired during period from 20th to 22nd. "D" Coy fired 8000 rds in response to a S.O.S. call. Adv Bn.H.Q. no change.	
ETRICOURT. V.3.b.8.8.	21/9/18		Location "A" "C" & "D" Coy H.Q's no change. "B" Coy H.Q. W.18.a.7.6. Bn.H.Q.Rear Moved East of Canal to V.3.b.8.8. near ETRICOURT Station. During the night "D" Coy relieved "B" Coy in the right sector. All guns of the latter company withdrawing to LOWLAND TRENCH where they remained on S.O.S. lines. Adv.B.H.Q. No change. 2/Lieut.F.Buckle joined Battalion as reinforcement from Base Depot and posted to "D" Coy. 22 O.R. joined Battalion as reinforcements from Base Depot. 2/Lieut.T.L.Smith K1 led in action. 2/Lieut.H.G.Head Wounded, 2/Lieut.R.A.Pleace 2/Lieut.A.R.K.J.Osbourn gassed. 3.O.R. Killed in action, 30. O.R. wounded.	
ETRICOURT Stn. V.3.b.8.8.	22/9/18.		Locations "A" Coy H.Q. W.9.c.7.0. "B" Coy H.Q. W.18.a.7.6. "C" Coy H.Q. W.15.d.1.8. "D" Coy H.Q. W.9.d.7.2. "C" Coy relieved "A" Coy in the left sector, the latter Coy taking over the barrage positions of the former. Gas projectors fired on selected areas. M.G.C. and artillery co-operating with harassing fire, 15000 rds being fired by "B" Coy. Adv.Bn.H.Q. No change. 7.O.R. awarded the Military Medal. 18 O.R. wounded in action. 1.O.R. died of wounds.	
ETRICOURT Stn. V.3.b.8.8.	23rd.		Locations "A" Coy H.Q. W.15.b.1.8. "B" - W.18.a.7.8. "C" - W.15.d.1.8. "D" - W.9.c.7.2. 8000 rds fired by "B" Coy on selected targets. Bn.H.Q. No change. A/Capt.H.E.Smith rejoined from leave and Maj.Musgrave gassed. 2/Lieut's.B.M.Thomas transferred to "A" Coy as 2.i/c. 1.O.R.Killed 4.O.R.wounded. 7.O.R.reported Missing. 1.O.R. died of wounds. Capt.C.G.Sheurr.RAMC.Rejoined from leave.	

Army Form C. 2118.

WAR DIARY
or
INTELLIGENCE SUMMARY. CONFIDENTIAL.
(Erase heading not required.)

Instructions regarding War Diaries and Intelligence Summaries are contained in F.S. Regs., Part II. and the Staff Manual respectively. Title pages will be prepared in manuscript.

Place	Date	Hour	Summary of Events and Information	Remarks and references to Appendices
ETRICOURT Stn. V.5.b.8.8.	24/9/18.		Locations unchanged, as for 23/9/18. Guns of "B" Coy fired 7500 rds on special targets. 1 gun "B" Coy out of action. Adv.Bn.H.Q. no change. 1.O.R.Killed in action. 1.O.R.wounded, 2.O.R. missing believed wounded. 2/Lieut.J.W.Jones "A" Coy admitted to hospital sick. Lieut.J.Storey."C" Coy proceeded on leave to U.K. 2/Lieut.D.G Latimer awarded the Military Cross. Sgt Moran J.MM. awarded the DCM.	
LE MESNIL EN ARROUAISE. U.5.a.1.4.	25th.		Division relieved in the line by the 21st Div. "A" & "B" Coys remained in the line in reserve positions to assist 21st Div. after relief by "D" & "A" Coys 21st Bn M.G.C. respectively. "C" & "D" Coys relieved by"C" & "B" Coys 21st Bn.M.G.C.respectively, staging at EQUANCOURT on returning to concentration point for Battalion, in LE MESNIL EN ARROUAISE. All "B" Echelons moved to concentration point during the morning. Adv.Bn.H.Q. no change.	
...do...	26th.		"A" & "B" Coys in the line. "C" & "D" Coys resting and reorganising. "D" Coy bathed. 2/Lieut.J.Hill joined Battalion as reinforcement and posted to "A" Coy. 59 O.R. joined Battalion as reinforcements from Base Depot. 2.O.R. rejoined from Base Depot. Adv.Battalion H.Q. no change. "A" Coy. Lieut.H.Jacobs, 2/Lieut.K.F.Earle, joined Battn. as reinforcements and posted to A/Capt. H.G.P.McIlroy 2/Lieut.J.R.Haughton joined Battalion as rel nforcement and was posted to "D" Coy. awarded the Military Cross. 2/Lieut.W.R.D.Looms "C" Coy proceeded on leave to U.K.	
...do...	27th.		Adv.Bn H.Q. not changed. 40 O.R. joined Battalion as reinforcements from Base Depot. Capt. C.G.Schurr R.A.M.C. evacuated sick.	
...do...	28th.		"A" & "B" Coy were withdrawn from line on enemy evacuating GOUZEAUCOURT.Adv.Bn.H.Q. closed and joined remainder of Battalion at U.5.a.1.4.	
;;;do...	29th.		Lieut.W.P.Allen.MC. "D" Coy rejoined from leave to U.K. General attack at YPRES by the Belgians, French and British captured HOUTHULSE Forest, and PASCHENDAELE Ridge. 1st & 3rd Armies with two American Divisions captured BOURLON WOOD and Village and advanced the line to within 1000 yds of CAMBRAI, establishing Bridge heads East of Canal at several points. American and French attack between VERDUN and RHEIMS reported going well.20,000 prisoners, 50,000 Turkish prisoners reported from PALESTINE.Allied forces in MACEDONIA advanced 40 miles	

A5834 Wt. W4973/M687 750,000 8/16 D. D. & L. Ltd. Forms/C.2118/13.

Army Form C. 2118.

WAR DIARY
or
INTELLIGENCE SUMMARY.   CONFIDENTIAL.
(Erase heading not required.)

Place	Date	Hour	Summary of Events and Information	Remarks and references to Appendices
	29th.		on 100 mile front, 10,000 prisoners reported. Armistice having been refused to BULGARIA she has asked for peace.	
LE MESNIL EN ARROUAISE. U.5.a.1.4.	30/9/18.		A/Major E?W.Davis, "A" Coy 2/Lieut.H.G.Rowles "B" Coy proceeded on leave to U.K. A. F.G.C.M. was held at H.Q. 52nd Inf Bde ROCQUIGNE for the trial of CSM.Hodge, and Pte Horne."D" Coy, on a charge of Drunkenness in each case. Enemy retired East of Canal de ESCAUT on Vth Corps front after evacuating GONNELIEU. Strength of Battalion........47 Officers. 812 Other Ranks.	

WAR DIARY
or
INTELLIGENCE SUMMARY.

Army Form C. 2118.

SECRET

Confidential.

WAR DIARY

OF

17th BATTALION M.G. CORPS

From 1.X.1918 to 31.X.1918

Army Form C. 2118.

WAR DIARY
or
INTELLIGENCE SUMMARY.   CONFIDENTIAL.

(Erase heading not required.)

17th BATTALION, OCTOBER 1918.

MACHINE GUN CORPS.

Strength of Battalion........47 Officers.
                              812 Other Ranks.

Place	Date	Hour	Summary of Events and Information	Remarks and references to Appendices
Sheet 57B.1/40,000. & 57B.NE.1/20,000. MESNIL-EN-ARROUAISE. U.5.a.1.4.	1/10/18.		Outposts have this day reached OSSUS and HONNECOURT on the Corps Front. Panic on the Bourse in BERLIN is reported. 17th Division is still in reserve, but prepared to move forward at 1 hrs notice.	
---do---	2/10/18.		Nothing of interest is recorded on the Corps Front. Enemy Machine Guns and snipers have been active from Trenches E of CANAL D'ESCAUT and rendering bridging futile. We are doing two hours training daily, paying special attention to Pack drill. The remainder of the day is being devoted to recreation. 2/Lieut. H.Wade. MC. "A" Company is promoted to Lieutenant. from 19/6/1918.	
---do---	3/10/18.		There is still no change on the Corps Front. Patrols crossed the Canal S of HONNECOURT and pushed forward through FRANQUEVILLE as far as the QUARRY - S.14.a.0.7, but here they were met by large numbers of the enemy and forced to retire to the Western side of the Canal. On this date the French captured ST QUENTIN. 32 O.R. joined Battn as reinforcements from Base Depot. 5.O.R.rejoined ex hospital. A/Capt.F.Hyde."C" Coy, 2/Lt.I.G.Jenkins,H.F.Morrell, H.S.Bolding, "B" Coy, proceeded on leave to U.K. A/Capt.& Adit. A.McInnes, proceeded to 14th Instructional Staff Course at M.G.T.C.Grantham.	

J Browning Major
Major Commanding 17 B" M.G.C.

Army Form C. 2118.

WAR DIARY
or
INTELLIGENCE SUMMARY.

Confidential.
(Erase heading not required.)

Instructions regarding War Diaries and Intelligence Summaries are contained in F. S. Regs., Part II. and the Staff Manual respectively. Title pages will be prepared in manuscript.

Place	Date	Hour	Summary of Events and Information	Remarks and references to Appendices
MESNIL-EN-ARROUAISE. U.5.a.1.4.	4/10/18.		This day and during the night the enemy retired from his positions E. of the Canal D'ESCAUT and the work of bridging and bridge improvement was energetically pushed forward to enable the 21st Division to follow him. Lieut.H.C.Wood, "D" Coy proceeded on leave to U.K.	
---do---	5/10/18.		Telephonic instructions were received from D.H.Q. that "C" & "D" Coys would move forward at 1230 and 1300 hrs respectively with 51st and 50th Infy Bdes and these moves were made accordingly, each Coy leaving its "B" Echelon with Battn.H.Q. "C" Company moved to W.12.b.0.5. "D" Coy to W.13.b.9.0. At 1300 hrs ordered were received from D.H.Q. for move of Battn.H.Q., "A" & "B" Coys to 0.30.d.8.5. area and march was commenced at 1515 hrs "B" Echelon of "C" & "D" Coys moving in rear. Route was via ETRICOURT-EQUANCOURT & FINS, and approximate locations were as follows:- Battn.H.Q. & "A" Coy W.14.d.5.6; "B" Coy, W.14.a.5.1; "C" & "D" Coys "B" Echelons W.14.d.2.8. Intelligence was received that the enemy was retiring along the whole of the Corps Front, pursued by 38th Div on right, 21st Div on left, 17th Div. to support 21st Div. on a One Brigade front, with boundaries as follows:- North BONNE ENFANCE FARM,incl.-0.22.d.0.0. South BONABUS FARM excl.0.30.c.0.0.-0.17.a.0.0. 7.O.R. proceeded on leave to U.K. and two O.R. to Paris.	
HEUDECOURT. W.14.d.5.6.	6/10/18.		38th and 21st Divisions were at 1700 hrs yesterday on the ground line AUBENCHAL-CATELET-NAUROI line-BONNE ENFANCE FARM with objectives as follows - 38th Div.MALINCOURT-High ground 0.27; 21st Div WALINCOURT - High GroundN.18.a.&.b. No move was made by Companies who were throughout the day held ready to move one hour after receipt of orders. During this time good progress was being made with the construction of bridges over the Canal D'ESCAUT, and tanks passed over a bridge at BANTEUX LOCKS M.25.d.9.5. at 1300 hrs on this date.	
---do---	7/10/18.		At 23 hrs yesterday two M.G.Coys were detailed by D.H.Q. to assist 21st Div. by barrage in an operation to be carried out on the 8th instant, and the C.O. accompanied by O's.C. "A" & "B" Companies visited O.C. 21st. Battalion, M.G.C. to make the necessary arrangements. "A" & "B" Coys moved up according at 4.p.m. and took up positions adjoining BONNE ENFANCE FARM in M.30.a. "C" & "D" Coys did not move.	

Army Form C. 2118.

WAR DIARY
or
INTELLIGENCE SUMMARY. Confidential.
(Erase heading not required.)

Instructions regarding War Diaries and Intelligence
Summaries are contained in F. S. Regs., Part II.
and the Staff Manual respectively. Title pages
will be prepared in manuscript.

Place	Date	Hour	Summary of Events and Information	Remarks and references to Appendices
HEUDECOURT W.14.d.5.6. R.32.a.5.8	8/10/18.		Zero Hour for the attack by the 21st Div. was 0515 hrs and "A" & "B" Coys each fired over 60,000 rounds chiefly on HARDISSART, MIDDLE & MALASSISE COPSES. They subsequently withdrew to reserve positions at M.33.c. and M.32.d.respectively. The attack had proved successful. "C" Coy attached to 51st.Bde closely followed up the 21st Div, moving first via GONNELIEU & BANTEUX to the Hindenberg Trench System just E. of the latter village and thence to GRATTEPANCHE FARM. "D" Coy with the 50th Bde followed in rear of the 51st Bde, marching to R.29.d.4.6. arriving about 1430 hrs, and thence to M.26.d.5.8. 2.0.R. "A" Coy wounded in action. Battalion H.Q. moved forward to R.32.a.5.8.	
R.32.a.5.8. VAUCELLES WOOD M.28.c.& N.16.a.9.5.	9/10/18.		0500 hrs. The 51st Bde passed through the 21st Div and continued the advance shortly after them. The Bde advanced with two Battalions leading and one Battalion in Support. One Section of "C" Company moved forward on the flank of each of the Leading Battalions, the other two being held in reserve and moving in rear of the support Battalion. At 0430 hrs Coy H.Q. moved to HURTEBISE FARM leaving there again for SELVIGNY at 0900 hrs. Here a short halt was made until 1300 hrs when the advance was continued to CAULLERY. At MONTIGNY some resistance was encountered by the leading Battalion, and a halt was called, ordered on the line gained at 1800 hrs. Outposts were established by the Infantry, and Sections remained in support of them. Meanwhile "D" Coy moved to HARDISSART FARM arriving about 1030 hrs and thence via N.21.d. to SELVIGNY. "A" Coy became attached to 52 Bde, and moved to HURTEBISE FARM, leaving there at 1800 hrs for SELVIGNY. "B" Coy moved forward to HARDISSART FARM where it was joined by Battalion Headquarters and all "B" Echelons who reached there at 1700 hrs after remaining for several hours en route in VAUCELLES WOOD, R.3B.a.area, having been cleared at 0700 hrs. At 1800 hrs Battalion H.Q. followed by "B" Coy again moved forward reaching N.16.a.9.5. at 1750 hrs. Where rations were at once dealt with, and sent out to Companies. 1 O.R. each "A" & "D" Coys died of wounds. The following notice appeared in Pt I orders. The following amounts received from Coys have this day been despatched to Hon.Secy.P.of W.Fund. M.G.C. Grantham. "H.Q." 112 francs; "B" - 379 francs; "C" - 331 francs; "D" 430 francs. Total 1252 francs.	
N.16.a.9.5. CLARI. 0.17.b.2.7. Ford Bn.HQ INCHY.J.22.d.8.8.	10/10/18.		50th Bde passed through the 51st Bde. "D" Coy moved to Cross Roads in O.5.d.moving forward thence at 0530 hrs, the former Bde having continued the advance. The high ground from J.12 - K.19.a. was reached Sections supporting the Infantry by direct overhead fire on to the Railway and high ground N.E. of the Railway. "D" Coy H.Q. were established at INCHY.J.22.b.2.6.	

J. Brown Major
Commanding 121 M.G. Bn

Army Form C. 2118.

WAR DIARY
or
INTELLIGENCE SUMMARY. Confidential.
(Erase heading not required.)

Instructions regarding War Diaries and Intelligence Summaries are contained in F.S. Regs., Part II. and the Staff Manual respectively. Title pages will be prepared in manuscript.

Place	Date	Hour	Summary of Events and Information	Remarks and references to Appendices
CIARI. 0.17.b.2.7. Ford Bn.H.Q. INCHI.J.22.d.8.8.	10/10/18.		Later, at about 1700 hrs, an attack was made on NEUVILL and direct overhead fire was carried out on targets appearing East of the Railway, in support of the Infantry advance. Infantry were, however, unable to occupy and consolidate the crest N.E. of the Railway, which had been their objective. "C" Coy remained in their positions at TRONQUOY - 0.5.d.central -O.11.d. Coy H.Q. moving from CAULLERY to MONTIGNY. "A" Coy took up ppsitions E. of BEAUMONT-INCHI. forming a defensive flank for the 52nd Bde. which remained in support of "A" Coy H.Q. established in J.27.b. "B" Coy moved forward to 0.17.b.2.7. and after a short rest, proceeded to battery positions in area J.12.a.-J.18.b.-K.13.d. establishing Coy H.Q. in INCHI at J.22.d.5.9. Battalion Headquarters moved forward to 0.17.b.2.7. At this stage the C.O. went forward to INCHI, establishing forward Battalion H.Q. there with 50th Bde H.Q. and later at Billet No.111 J.22.d.8.8. 5.O.R.proceeded on leave to U.K.	
---do---	11/10/18.		About 1760 hrs 50th Bde again attacked NEUVILL. "B" Coy fired 30,000 rounds barrage fire in support on area K.b.b., K.9.a. One section of "D" Coy was detailed to follow on each flank and to consolidate line of the Railway, remaining two sections supported the attack by overhead fire. On word being received that objectives had not been reached, sections were withdrawn to their original positions, to cover the consolidation of the support outpost line, along the River SELLE. 50th Bde was withdrawn about 0300 hrs. "C" Coy moved up to INCHI after dark, to take up barrage positions for an attack by the 52nd Bde on the following morning. "A" Coy withdrew from the flank positions occupied the previous day and concentrated in BEAUMONT, preparatory to assisting in the attack. 4 O.R. "B" Coy, 1 O.R. "C" Coy, 3 O.R. "D" Coy wounded. 5 O.R. proceeded on leave to U.K. Lieut. E.J.C.Cubberley H.Q. rejoined from leave to U.K.	
---do--- TRONQUOY. P.1.a.0.7.	12/10/18.		52nd Bde attacked NEUVILL at 0500 hrs. On the left Manchesters reached position in K.2.b. and E.26.c. accompanied by two sections of "A" Coy. On the right, The Duke of Wellingtons were held up and the other two sections of "A" Coy who supported them took up defensive positions on forward slope 500 yds S. of River. Heavy counter attack at 1600 hrs drove the left flank almost back to the river, and forced the two sections on that flank to retire with the infantry, after exhausting all their ammunition. Five guns and seven tripods were lost as the result. The three remaining guns of these two sections held on the	

(A7093). Wt.W12630/M1293. 75,000. 1/17. D.D. & L., Ltd. Forms/C.2118A.

Army Form C. 2118.

WAR DIARY
or
INTELLIGENCE SUMMARY.   Confidential.
(Erase heading not required.)

Instructions regarding War Diaries and Intelligence Summaries are contained in F.S. Regs., Part II. and the Staff Manual respectively. Title pages will be prepared in manuscript.

Place	Date	Hour	Summary of Events and Information	Remarks and references to Appendices
TRONQUOY. P.I.a.O.7.	12/10/18.		bank just N. of the River until relieved and withdrew to BEAUMONT, with the remainder of the Company. "C" Coy supported the attack with barrage fire from positions about at J.18.central and "B" Coy from same positions as on the previous day. "D" Coy was withdrawn to INGHI about 2000 hrs. Battalion H.Q.Rear moved forward at 0930 hrs, to TRONQUOY. P.I.a.O.7. Locations:- "A" H.Q. J.21.d.80.80;"B" - J.22.d.7.8.;"C" - J.22.d.4.2;"D" Coy J.22.b.3.5. Battalion H.Q.Advanced, No.change. Lieut.J.Storey "C" Coy and Lieut.A.W.Higgins, "B" Coy struck off strength on proceeding to England for Tour of duty at home. 1.O.R. "A" Coy killed in action, 5 O.R. "D" Coy wounded.	

P.I.a.O.7.	13/10/18.		A thorough reconnaissance was made and sections of "B" & "C" Coys disposed as follows in order ot provide for the M.G.Defence of the Divisional front.
			Right Sector. i.e.One Section,Trenches K.13.b.
			    K.13.b.80.30.-Northern End of Ravine.
			  Two sections, J.24.a.(in reserve)
			  One section, J.12.b.
			Left Sector.
			  One section, J.12.d.&.K.7.c.
			  Two sections. J.17.b.(reserve)
			"A" & "D" Coys remained in INCHY - BEAUMONT.
			26.O.R. "D" Coy joined Battalion as reinforcements from Base Depot.
			2.O.R. "A" Coy Killed in action, 4.O.R. "A" Coy wounded, 1 O.R."A" Coy wounded and Missing, 4.O.R."A" Coy Missing, 1.O.R. "C" Coy wounded.	

Forward.INCHY. J.22.d.8.8. & 14/10/18 Rear.TRONQUOY.18/10/18. P.I.a.O.7.			"A" & "D" Companies remained in BEAUMONT-INCHY resting and reorganising. "B" & "C" Companies continued to hold the left and right sectors of the Divisional front at NEUVILLY until the 17th when "C" Coy was withdrawn to INCHY about 18.00 hrs, the two forward sections being relieved by two sections of "B" Coy. Lieut.G.T.Fraser, "B" Coy) 2/Lieut.W.R.D.Looms."C" "H") Rejoined from leave to U.K. 16th Octr. 2/Lieut.J.A.Hill, "A" Coy. wounded in action, 16th. 3 O.R. "C" Coy, 1 O.R. "D" Coy Killed in action; 1 O.R. "B" Coy, 3 O.R. "C" Coy 6 O.R. "D" Coy wounded in action. 16 O.R. proceeded on leave to U.K. 2 O.R. "B" & 6 O.R. "C" Coys wounded gas.	

Army Form C. 2118.

WAR DIARY
or
INTELLIGENCE SUMMARY

CONFIDENTIAL.

(Erase heading not required.)

Instructions regarding War Diaries and Intelligence Summaries are contained in F. S. Regs., Part II. and the Staff Manual respectively. Title pages will be prepared in manuscript.

Place	Date	Hour	Summary of Events and Information	Remarks and references to Appendices
Forward. INCHY. J.22.d.8.8. Rear. TRONQUOY. P.1.a.0.7.	19/10/18.		"A" & "D" Coys moved forward to NEUVILLY SECTOR preparatory to supporting 50th and 51st Inf.Bdes. "B" Coy took up battery positions in TRENCH running through K.7.c. and K.8.a. "C" Coy moved up to Battery positions near RAMBOURLIEUX FARM. Lieut.R.G.Bond "C" Coy proceeded on leave to U.K. Major E.W.Davis. "A" Coy) 2/Lt.H.G.Rowles. "B") rejoined from leave to U.K. 12 O.R. joined Battalion as reinforcements from Base Depot.	
---do---	20/10/18.		Attack on Ridge E. of NEUVILLY commenced at 02.00 hrs. 50th Bde led with sections of "D" Coy supporting 6th Dorsets on left and 7th East Yorks on Right. They assisted in consolidating the Ridge and Railway E. of NEUVILLY Enemy counter attacks failed to reach this line. "C" Coy after firing barrages moved forward on pack and took up positions on high ground E. of NEUVILLY to repel counter attacks. Later 51st Bde passed through 50th Bde and took AMERVAL and AMERVAL RIDGE supported by "A" Coy; "B" Coy after firing barrage withdrew to reserve positions in Road J.17.b. "C" Coy Headquarters for the attack were established at J.18.a.5.3. till 21.00 hrs when they moved into NEUVILLY, and on crossing the R.SELLE the Coy came under the orders of the 51st Bde. "D" Coy H.Q. for the attack were at K.8.d.1.5. 2/Lieut.T.H.Waddell. "A" Coy) Wounded in action. Lieut.A.H.Jacobs. "A" ") 2/Lieut.H.Roberts "D" Coy proceeded on leave to U.K. 1 O.R. "C" Coy Killed. 1 O.R. "A" , 2 O.R. "B" , 2 O.R. "C" & 4 O.R. "D" Coy wounded. 1 O.R. "H.Q." Died of wounds. 8 O.R. proceeded on leave to U.K.	
---do---	21/10/18.		50th Bde was relieved by 52nd Bde. "C" Coy was withdrawn to INCHY. 2 sections at K.3.b.8.0. and K.3.a.8.2. having been relieved by "D" Coy, and the remaining two sections by "A" Coy. "B" Coy was also withdrawn to INCHY. Capt. F.Hyde, "C" Coy.) rejoined from leave to U.K. Lieut.C.J.Dewey, "D") Lieut.E.H.F.Kelly joined Battalion as reinforcement from Base Depot and was posted to "C" Coy. 14 O.R. joined Battalion as reinforcements ex Base Depot. 1 O.R. "D" Coy wounded.	
---do---	22/10/18.		On relief of 17th Divn by 21st Divn. "A" & "D" Coys after relief by 21st M.G.Bn. withdrew to INCHY SUCRERIE completing this move by 02.00 hrs 23rd instant. Major E.W.Davis "A" Coy struck off strength on proceeding to U.K. for six months tour of duty at home. 2/Lt.T.Rawlinson "B" Coy proceeded on leave to U.K.	

J.Gorring Major 17 Bn R. Welsh

Army Form C. 2118.

WAR DIARY
or
INTELLIGENCE SUMMARY.
Confidential.

(Erase heading not required.)

Instructions regarding War Diaries and Intelligence Summaries are contained in F.S. Regs., Part II. and the Staff Manual respectively. Title pages will be prepared in manuscript.

Place	Date	Hour	Summary of Events and Information	Remarks and references to Appendices
INCHY.J.23.d.8.8.	23/10/18.		"B" Coy became attached to 51st Inf Bde and moved forward to AMERVAL FARM en route for OVILLERS AREA. Other Coys did not move. Bn. Rear H.Q. and All "B" Echelons moved to INCHY, joining up with Bn.H.Q.(Forward). 2.O.R. "A" and 1 O.R. "B" Coy wounded gas.	
---do---	24/10/18.		No movr. Lieut. P.B.LUCAS joined Battalion as reinforcement and was posted to "A" Coy. Lieut.W.B.Martin, "A" Coy proceeded on leave to U.K. 2/Lt.I.C.Jenkins, and 2/Lt.H.F.Morrell "B" Coy rejoined from leave to U.K. 12 O.R. joined Battalion as reinforcements ex Base Depot.	
---do---	25/10/18.		No move. 2/Lt A.S.Bolding, "B" Coy and Lt.H.Wood "D" Coy rejoined from leave to U.K. Lieut.Colonel W.A.Grierson, DSO, proceeded on leave to U.K. 9 O.R. proceeded on leave.	
INCHY.J.22.d.8.8. VENDIGIES(Forward) Rear.OVILLERS E.23.b.8.1.	26/10/18.		Bn.H.Q.(Forward) moved to VENDIGIES on relief by 17th of 21st Div. 52nd Bde took over the line, 50th Bde went to POIX du NORD and 51st Bde to VENDIGIES. "A" & "B" Coys became attached to 52nd Bde and took over the forward positions from the 21st M.G.Bn. establishing their Coy H.Q. in POIX du NORD. "C" Coy relieved positions on the high ground between VENDIGIES and POIX du NORD with two sections, the other two sections occupying billets close to Coy H.Q. in VENDIGIES. "D" Coy occupied billets in VENDIGIES standing at 30 minutes notice to occupy village defences. Battn Rear H.Q. with all "B" Echelons moved forward to OVILLERS - E.23.b.8.1.	
Forward VENDIGIES. Rear.OVILLERS E.23.b.8.1.	27/10/18.		Reorganisation of the M.G Defences of the Divisional front took place "A" Coy taking the Left Sector and "B" Coy the Right. S.O.S.Lines were laid out. During the night the two sections of "C" Coy occupying positions were withdrawn to Billets in VENDIGIES. "D" Coy did not move. 10 O.R. joined Battalion as reinforcements from Base Depot. 2.O.R. "A" Coy and 1 O.R. "B" Coy wounded.	
---do---	28/10/18.		"A" "B" & "C" Coys didnot move, but guns of "A" Coy assisted an attack by the Div. on our Right by harassing fire. "D" Coy moved up into reserve positions three sections occupying the Ridge E. of POIX du NORD the fourth occupying billets in the village where new Coy H.Q. were established. "D" Coy then became attached to 50th Bde. 8.O.R. proceeded on leave to U.K. 3 O.R. "B" & 2 O.R. "A" Coy wounded.	
Forward VENDIGIES. Rear OVILLERS E.23.b.8.1. INCHY.	29/10/18.		17th Div was relieved by 21st Div. All Coys Bn.H.Q. and "B" Echelons withdrawn on relief to INCHY where all four companies were billetted in a factory close to INCHY Station Route VENDIGIES. AMERVAL FARM and NEUVILLY. "C" Coy was awarded the M.C.	

Army Form C. 2118.

WAR DIARY
or
INTELLIGENCE SUMMARY.
Confidential.

(Erase heading not required.)

Instructions regarding War Diaries and Intelligence Summaries are contained in F. S. Regs., Part II. and the Staff Manual respectively. Title pages will be prepared in manuscript.

Place	Date	Hour	Summary of Events and Information	Remarks and references to Appendices
INCHY.	30/10/18. 31/10/18.		Both days were spent in bathing and cleaning up, checking and cleaning guns and equipment. 2/Lieut.L.Meeson, and Lt.W.Glen joined Battalion as reinforcements ex Base Depot and were posted to "A" & "C" Coys respectively. 2/Lieut.S.Richards, R.E. attached to Battalion for duty as Signalling Officer. 102155.Cpl.Jones,O."D" Coy and 156185.Pte.Potts,J. "A" Coy awarded the M.M. S U M M A R Y, O C T O B E R,1918:- Number of Guns destroyed/during month.... 5. by shell fire captured by enemy - 5. Casualties....Officers....Killed. 1. Wounded,2. Other Ranks..Killed. 2. Wounded, 50. Wounded & Missing. 2. Died of wounds 4. Wounded gas. 26. Strength of Battalion at 31/10/18:- Officers........... 46. Other Ranks....... 792.	

J Browning Major
for Major Crosby 1/4th R.W.C.C.

Army Form C. 2118.

WAR DIARY
or
INTELLIGENCE SUMMARY.
(Erase heading not required.)

Confidential.

17th Battalion, Machine Gun Corps.

N O V E M B E R 1 9 1 8.

Summary of Events and Information

Strength of Battalion:...... 46 officers,
792 Other Ranks.

Place	Date	Hour	Summary of Events and Information	Remarks and references to Appendices
Sheet 57B.1/40,000. INCHY.	1/11/18.		Battalion still resting in Billets at INCHY.	
INCHY. Ford: VENDIGIES. Rear: OVILLERS. E.23.b.8.1.	2/11/18.		"A" & "B" Coys to VENDIGIES AREA establishing H.Q. at E.12.d.central and F.7.c.1.5.respectively. "C" Coy relieved "G" Coy 21st M.G.Bn in the line, and had its Companies with the 152nd Inf.Bde. area, establishing Coy H.Q. at POIX-DU-NORD. Battalion H.Q. (Ford) moved to VENDIGIES, and Rear to OVILLERS. Lieuts. F. Watson, and W.S.Hutton joined Battalion as reinforcements from Base Depot, and were posted to B.& C.Coys respectively. 2/Lieut.R.F.Trethewey proceeded to Vth Corps Gas Course at MONTIGNY. Lieut.H.Wade MC "A" Company, killed in action. 40 O.R. joined Battalion as reinforcements ex Base Depot.	
Ford: VENDIGIES. Rear: OVILLERS. E.23.b.8.1.	3/11/18.		At dusk "C" & "D" Coys took up selected battery positions in readiness to support an attack by the 52nd Bde on the following morning. 1st objective was the Western Edge of the FORET de MORMAL. Battalion Ford H.Q. moved into POIX-DU-NORD. 3 O.R. joined Battalion as reinforcements from Base Depot.	
-----do-----	4/11/18.		"C" & "D" Coys each fired 25,000 rounds on the objective in the first attack.This attack was successful. "C" & "D" Coys later being withdrawn to billets in POIX-DU-NORD, 2 sections of "A" Coy which had also been attached to 52nd Bde for moving forward with the infantry, had assisted by giving covering fire into FUTOY. These two sections	

Army Form C. 2118.

WAR DIARY
or
INTELLIGENCE SUMMARY.
Confidential.

(Erase heading not required.)

Instructions regarding War Diaries and Intelligence Summaries are contained in F.S. Regs., Part II. and the Staff Manual respectively. Title pages will be prepared in manuscript.

Place	Date	Hour	Summary of Events and Information	Remarks and references to Appendices
Ford:POIX-DU-NORD, Rear.OVILLERS E.23.b.8.1. Rear:POIX-DU-NORD.	5/11/18.		later took up positions on the FUTOY Road. The remaining two sections of "A" Coy went forward with the 51st Inf.Bde to the second objective, which was as follows:- AVESNES-ST REMY CHAUSSEE-PONT-SUR-SAMBRE-BAVAY Road. This objective also was gained and positions taken up, on the flanks. 50th Bde, supported by "B" Coy then went forward and continued the advance through 51st Bde, with objective N.&.S.Road T.15.a.&.c.-T.21s.-T.20.b.&.d. About 1400 hrs, 7th East Yorks,(½ left Battalion) was held up by enemy M.G.fire on S .181d.central, 2/Lieut.H.A.Disney. M.C.DCM. succeeded in capturing the 2 guns which were delaying the infantry, and brought them into action on the dense wood running through T.7.c. This enabled the advance to continue. First dispositions - 4 guns in position at S.18.b.5.8. and S.18.b.8.5. forming defensive flank to cover counter-attack from N.E; two sections at S.18.c.5.3.-S.18.c.5.4.-S.18.c.5.5.-S.18.c.4.3.-S.18.c.3.3.-S.18.c.3.5.-S.18.c.4.5.-remaining section in defensive positions at T.13.c.area. Lieut.Col.E.G.Mercer. CMG, attached to Battalion, together with Bat m.n. 2/Lieut.E.Newton, wounded in action, also 2/Lieut.H F.Morrell, of "A" Coy. 3.0.R."A" Coy, 2.0.R."B" Coy 1.0.R."C" Coy, Killed in action; 16 O.R."A" Coy, 6.0.R."B" Coy 4."C" Coy and 3 "D" Coy wounded in action; 1.0.R."A" Coy wounded and remained at duty.	
POIX-DU-NORD LA TETE NOIRE.	6/11/18.		"A" Coy concentrated in BUTOY, and "B" Coy in LOCQUIGNOL on 21st Div passing through 17th Div. "C" & "D" Coys did not move. Battalion H.Q.Rear moved forward to POIX-DU-NORD and joined up with Battalion H.Q.Ford. A/Major.J.S.Gowring.M.C. proceeded on one month's leave to U.K.; A/Major.F.J..A.Dibd n.MC took over duties of 2.I.c; Lieut.F.Watson transferred from "B" to "A" Coy.	
LA-TETE-NOIRE. BERLAIMONT. U.20.d.8.6.	7/11/18.		The following moves were carried out:- "A" Coy FUTOY to LA-TETE-NOIRE with 51st Bde Group; Battalion H.Q. with "C" & "D" Coys POIX-DU-N°RD to LA-TETE-NOIRE. "B" Coy did not move. Orders had been issued for an attack by the 21st Division on the morning of the following day and the role of the 17th Div. was to follow close in rear. It was anticipated that this attack would meet with little, if any, opposition, and this proved to be correct. 17th Division passed through 21st Div, and the following moves were carried out.- Battalion H.Q. to BERLAIMONT; "A" Coy with 52nd Bde to BERLAIMONT; "B" Coy with 50th Bde to BACHANT: "C" & "D" Coys with 51st Bde to AULNO R and BACHANT respectively. Lieut.R.G.Bond "C" Coy rejoined from leave to U.K. M/Capt.F.H.Arnold, "B" Coy proceeded to Machine Gun School, GAMIERS for 60th Ordinary M.G.Course.	

A5834 Wt. W4973/M687 750,000 8/16 D.D. & L. Ltd. Forms/C.2118/13.

Army Form C. 2118.

WAR DIARY
or
INTELLIGENCE SUMMARY.   Confidential.
(Erase heading not required.)

Instructions regarding War Diaries and Intelligence Summaries are contained in F.S. Regs., Part II. and the Staff Manual respectively. Title pages will be prepared in manuscript.

Place	Date	Hour	Summary of Events and Information	Remarks and references to Appendices
BERLAIMONT U.20.d.8.6. AULNOLE.	8/11/18.		Battalion H.Q. moved to AULNOLE, followed by "A" Coy; 51st Bde attacked and captured LIMONT-FONTAINE, "D" Coy firing overhead in support of the attack, and later moving forward Coy H.Q. to that village. "B" & "C" Coys did not move.	
AULNOLE.	9/11/18.		51st Bde attacked early in the morning and again at 1640 hrs to capture the line of the MAUBERGE-AVESNES Road. Both attacks were held up by M.G.fire and were unsuccessful. At 21.30 hrs patrols reported that the enemy had vacated this line, which was then occupied. 51st Bde were later relieved by 52nd Bde. "B" Coy moved forward with 50th Bde to LIMONT-FONTAINE. 13 O.R.proceeded on leave to U.K.	
--do--	10/11/18.		Attack was resumed at Dawn, and village of BEHUFORT occupied. "D" Coy moved forward Coy H.Q. to that village. 23.O.R.proceeded on leave to U.K.	
--do--	11/11/18.		Armistice came into effect at 1100 hrs, and "B" & "D" Coys moved back to BERLAIMONT.	
--do-- ENGLEFONTAINE.	12/11/18.		Battalion moved with 50th Bde Group to ENGLEFONTAINE via SASSIGNIES-B.18.central,-B.10.central-B.14.d-B.1.central-Route de HECQ. (Sheets 51.SW.1/20,000, 57A.1/40,000)	
ENGLEFONTAINE BERTRY.	13/11/18.		Battalion moved with 50th Bde Group to BERTRY via CROIX-MONTAY-MAUROIS.(Sheet 57B.1/40,000) 2/Lieut.R.E.Trethewey rejoined from Course at VTh Corps Gas School.	
BERTRY.	14/11/18.		2/Lieut.W.Donnelly.R.E. became attached to Battalion as Signalling Officer, 2/Lieut. S.Richards.returning to Division H.Q.R.E. for duty. Lieut.W.B.Martin rejoined ex leave to U.K. 83 O.R. joined Battalion as reinforcements ex Base Depot.	
--do--	15/11/18.		2/Lieut.H.Waddell. "A" Coy, previously wounded in action, rejoined Battalion as reinforcement ex Base Depot. Lieut.E.J.C.Cubberley struck off strength on proceeding to U.K, for tour of duty at M.G.T.C. 40.O.R.joined Battalion as reinforcements ex Base Depot.	
--do--	16/11/18.		Lieut.Col.W.A.Grierson.DSO, rejoined from leave to U.K. 2/Lieut.T.C.Dowse attached to Battalion H.Q. ex "A" Coy for duty as Battalion Transport Officer.Lieut.F.Watson, "A" Coy transferred to "D" Coy. 7.O.R.proceeded on leave to U.K.	

Army Form C. 2118.

WAR DIARY
or
INTELLIGENCE SUMMARY.
Confidential.

(Erase heading not required.)

Place	Date	Hour	Summary of Events and Information	Remarks and references to Appendices
BERTRY.	17/11/18.		Church Parade for Battalion at 1000 hrs. During the afternoon "A" "B" & "C" Coys bathed. A/Capt.A.McInnes, Adjt., returned from Staff Instructional Course, M.G.T.C.Grantham.	
--do--	18/11/18.		All Companies spent the afternoon collecting salvage. 15 O.R. proceeded on leave to U.K. F.G.C.M. was held at BERTRY for trial of 15138.Sgt.Hogge E, on charge of Drunkenness.	
--do--	19/11/18.		775 limber loads of scrap material, metal, artillery empties ordnance stores, etc, were sent to Different dumps. Salvage work was continued in the morning, as a result of time spent in this way.	
--do--	20/11/18.		U/L/Cpl.Caley."B" Coy awarded the Military Medal.	
--do--	21/11/18.		2/Lieut.J.W.Jones, "B" Coy, previously evacuated sick, rejoined as reinforcement ex Base Depot. Lieut.D.A.K.Stephen joined Battalion as reinforcement and was posted to "B" Coy. Lieut.F.Perch. "A" Coy, and 2/Lieut.H.G.Holloran, "C" Coy proceeded on leave to U.K. 22 O.R. joined Battalion as reinforcements from Base Depot.	
--do--	22-11-18.		Lieut.Col.E.G.Mercer,GMG, attached to Battalion for instruction, proceeded to take over Command of 58th Battalion, Machine Gun Corps. T/2/Lieut.D.G.Latimer.MC. promoted to T/Lieut. London Gazette, 26-10-18.	
--do--	23-11-18.		2/Lieut.W.R.D.Loomis, "C" Coy proceeded to Officers Rest House, PARIS PLAGE.	
--do--	24-11-18.		Church Parades. Battalion Rugby Team played 7th East Yorks Regt in the afternoon, Result, Nil-Nil.	
--do--	25-11-18.		Salvage work, 26 limber loads of material removed to various dumps.	
--do--	26-11-18.		Battalion Inspected by Divisional General.	
--do--	27-11-18.		Usual parades. 2/Lieut.A.C.Wylde, proceeded on leave to U.K.	
--do--	28-11-18.		2/Lieut.M.W.Penman proceeded to 1st Refresher Educational Course at DOURIEZ.	
--do--	29-11-18.		Parades, as usual.	
--do--	30-11-18.		Inspection of Companies by C.O. A/Major H.E.Smith.MC. granted short leave to Paris.	

Strength of Battalion........ 46 officers, 863 Other Ranks.

Army Form C. 2118.

WAR DIARY
or
INTELLIGENCE SUMMARY.   Confidential.
(Erase heading not required.)

17th Battalion, Machine Gun Corps.   War Diary for the month of

DECEMBER 1918.

Strength of Battalion at December 1st,........47 Officers,
                                               850 Other Ranks.

-x-x-x-x-x-x-x-x-x-x-x-x-x-x-x-x-x-x-x-x-

Place	Date	Hour	Summary of Events and Information	Remarks and references to Appendices
BERTRY.	1-12-18.		Divine Services. T/Lieut.H.Kennedy reinforcement from Base Depot 30-11-18, posted to "A" Company.	
...do...	2-12-18.		Salvaging area. 17 limber loads were removed to respective dumps.	
...do...	3-12-18.		Salvaging. - 5 limber loads. A/Capt.F.H.Arnold rejoined from Machine Gun Course G.H.Q.M.G.School, Camiers.	
...do...	4-12-18.		Informal review by His Majesty the King, on LE CATEAU Road at J.30.b. The day was wet.	
...do...	5-12-18.		Usual parades. 2/Lieut.L.Moeson took over duties of Sports Officer.	
...do...	6-12-18.		2 hrs Route March. 2/Lieut.R.E.Tretheway "D" Company admitted sick. Lieut.D.G Latimer, M.C "B" Company leave to U.K. 7-12-18 to 21-12-18.	
...do...	7-12-18.		General cleaning up of billets etc preparatory to move. Major H.E.Tobb joined Battalion as reinforcement from Base Depot. 2/Lieut "D" Company H.E. Smith A/Major.H.E.Smith rejoined from short leave to Paris.	
MASNIERES.	8-12-18.		Battalion left BERTRY at 0950 hrs and marched to MASNIERES arriving at 1500 hrs Dinners were immediately served on arrival. Billets were fairly comfortable.	

Army Form C. 2118.

WAR DIARY
or
INTELLIGENCE SUMMARY.   Confidential.
(Erase heading not required.)

Instructions regarding War Diaries and Intelligence Summaries are contained in F. S. Regs., Part II. and the Staff Manual respectively. Title pages will be prepared in manuscript.

Place	Date	Hour	Summary of Events and Information	Remarks and references to Appendices
HERMIES.	9-12-18.		Battalion left MASNIERES at 1000 hrs and marched to HERMIES, arriving at 1400 hrs. and were billeted in tents.	
BEUGNATRE, CAMBRAI Road.	10-12-18.		Battalion left HERMIES at 1000 hrs and marched to FAVREUIL, (BEUGNATRE) via BAPAUME-CAMBRAI Road, arriving at 1530 hrs. It rained all day. Billets were old Nissen Huts.	
ALBERT.	11-12-18.	1600 hrs.	Battalion left BEUGNATRE at 0845 hrs, and marched to ALBERT, via LE SARS, arriving at 1600 hrs. It rained all morning. Billets, - tents, situate near Railway Station.	
LAHOUSSOYE.	12-12-18.		Battalion left ALBERT at 0947 hrs, and marched to LA HOUSSOYE arriving at 1300 hrs. It rained all day. Billets fairly comfortable.	
BRETILLY-SUR-SOMME	13-12-18.		Battalion left LA HOUSSOYE at 0825 hrs, and marched through AMIENS to BRETILLY. A halt was made outside AMIENS for an hour, - dinners were served - arrived at BRETILLY 1700 hrs. Very good billets.	
LE QUESNOY-SUR-AIRAINES.	14-12-18.		Battalion left BRETILLY at 0930 hrs and marched to LE QUESNOY SUR AIRAINES, via SOUES arriving at 1300 hrs, where advanced Billeting party which consisted of Lieut.W.P.Allen and 2/Lieut.H.G.Rowles, had everything prepared. NOTE. DURING THE WHOLE SEVEN DAYS' MARCH ONLY ONE MARCH CASUALTY WAS REPORTED. 60 Other ranks joined Battalion as reinforcements from Base Depot. 2/Lieut.H.Holland joined as reinforcement and was posted to "B" Coy.	
...do...	15-12-18.		Cleaning up.	
...do...	16-12-18.		Further cleaning up of all vehicles, harness and gun gear. 2/Lieut. C.E.Gowers granted leave to U.K. from 16-12-18, to 30-12-18. A/Major T.S.Gowring, Lieut.F.Perch, 2/Lieut.H.G.Holman and 2/Lieut.A.C.Wylde all rejoined from leave.	
...do...	17-12-18.		Further cleaning up. Baths, etc.	
...do...	18-12-18.		Usual parades. Lecture on Agriculture and Agricultural Reconstruction was delivered by a Lecturer from G.H.Q at 1100 hrs. 130 all ranks attended.	
...do...	19-12-18.		Companies at the disposal of company Commanders.	

COMMANDING 17 BATTN. M.G.C.

Army Form C. 2118.

WAR DIARY
or
INTELLIGENCE SUMMARY.   Confidential.

(Erase heading not required.)

Instructions regarding War Diaries and Intelligence Summaries are contained in F.S. Regs., Part II and the Staff Manual respectively. Title pages will be prepared in manuscript.

Place	Date	Hour	Summary of Events and Information	Remarks and references to Appendices
LE QUESNOY SUR AIRAINES	20-12-18		Lieut.(A/Major) H.G.P.McIlroy, and Lieut.(A/Capt) F.Watson, both of "D" Company, to wear the badges of acting rank.	
...do...	21-12-18		Xmas Dinner. C.O. thanked the Officers of the Battalion for contributions towards Battalion Xmas Dinner. 2/Lieut.M.W.Perman rejoined from Educational Refresher Course.	
...do...	22-12-18		Divine Services. Battalion Rugby Team played 9th Battalion Duke of Wellington Regt at METIGNY, and was beaten by 15 points to Nil. Lieut.W.P.Allen detached at R.O.D. AURRUICQ.	
...do...	23-12-18		30 Other ranks reinforcements arrived under conducting officer, Lieut.Mason, from the Base. 44 O.R. were reported Missing.	
...do...	24-12-18		40 of the O.R. reinforcements arrived. Lieut.D.G.Latimer reported from leave.	
...do...	25-12-18		The Battalion Christmas Dinner was given in the large Dining Hall in two sittings. Two free cinema performances were given by the courtesy of the 4th Army Signal School Officers. Shows at 1400 hrs and 1700 hrs. Officers v Sergeants Football Match at 1000 hrs, result, Sergts 5 goals, Officers 2.	
...do...	26-12-18		No parades. Whist Drives at 5.p.m. in Large Hall.	
...do...	27-12-18		Companies Ceremonial Drill.	
...do...	28-12-18		Usual parades.	
...do...	29-12-18		Divine Services. Inter-section Football matches played off all day.	
...do...	30-12-18		Usual parades. Battalion Officers Mess inaugurated successfully in the Chateau.	
...do...	31-12-18		Usual parades. Strength of Battalion at the close of the year,...... 49 Officers, 851 Other ranks.	

-x-x-x-x-x-x-x-x-x-x-x-x-

[signature]
LIEUT. COLONEL,
COMMANDING 17 BATTN. M.G. CORPS.

Army Form C. 2118.

WAR DIARY
or
INTELLIGENCE SUMMARY.
Confidential.
(Erase heading not required.)

17th Battalion,

MACHINE GUN CORPS.

-x-x-x-x-x-x-x-x-x-x-x-x-x-x-x-x-x-x-x-x-x-x-x-x-x-

JANUARY. 1919.

Strength of Battalion at January 1st, 1919......Officers..... 49.
                                                Other Ranks. 850.

Place	Date	Hour	Summary of Events and Information	Remarks and references to Appendices
LE QUESNOY SUR AIRAINES	1/1/19		Battalion paraded as strong as possible,(less Transport) for Ceremonial Drill. Officers were mounted. Capt. E.M.Thomas to be acting Major, Lieut.W.B.Martin to be acting Captain.	
...do...	2/1/19		Companies at the disposal of Company Commanders. Lieut.C.E.Gowers rejoined from leave. No.68490.Cpl.Llewellyn.C. "G" Coy. mentioned in despatches 31-12-18.	
...do...	3/1/19		Battalion,(less Transport) paraded as strong as possible for Ceremonial Drill. Officers were mounted.	
...do...	4/1/19		Companies attended Divine Service in the Cinema Hut at 1000 hrs. Major.E.M.Thomas granted leave to U.K. from 3-1-19 to 17-1-19.	
...do...	5/1/19		Companies were at the disposal of Company Commanders. The usual parades and fatigues were carried out. The Battalion were paid. Fire precautions were taken and fire buckets issued to each billet.	
...do...				

COMMANDING 17 BATTN. M.G. CORPS

Army Form C. 2118.

WAR DIARY
or
INTELLIGENCE SUMMARY.
Confidential.
(*Erase heading not required.*)

Instructions regarding War Diaries and Intelligence Summaries are contained in F. S. Regs., Part II. and the Staff Manual respectively. Title pages will be prepared in manuscript.

Place	Date	Hour	Summary of Events and Information	Remarks and references to Appendices
LE QUESNOY SUR AIRAINES.	6/1/19.		Companies were at the disposal of Company Commanders. All men of the Battalion were bathed and received a clean change of washing. A Debate was held in the Cinema Hut, Subject, Should Railways be Nationalised. For:- Capt. F.H.Arnold, and Sgt Davis, Against:- Lieut.Looms, and L/Cpl.Tanner,B.G. Education classes were held.	
...do...	7/1/19.		Companies at the disposal of Company Commanders. The usual fatigues were carried out. Permanent fatigue party was detailed to erect stables. A Lecture was delivered by Capt. & Adjt., A.McIntee at 1000 hrs in the Cinema Hut. Subject, "Evolution of Commerce". The usual Education Classes were held in the Cinema Hut.	
...do...	8/1/19.		Companies at the disposal of Company Commanders. The usual parades and fatigues were carried out. All animals on strength of the Battalion were classified. Lecture by Lieut.H.Roberts on "The Constitution of the British Government".	
...do...	9/1/19.		Companies at the disposal of company commanders. Lieut.E.M.F.Kelly proceeded to U.K. for demobilisation, and struck off strength of Battalion. 2/Lieut.H.C.Maschwitz granted leave to U.K. from 9-1-19. to 23-1-19. Lecture given in the Cinema Hut by Major Monkton, Divisional Education Officer. Subject, "The causes and Issues of the War".	
...do...	10/1/19.		Companies at the disposal of company commanders. A Whist Drive was held in the Cinema Hut at 1700 hrs. The usual parades carried out.	
...do...	11/1/19.		Companies attended Divine Service in the Cinema Hut at 1000 hrs.	
...do...	12/1/19.		Companies at the disposal of Company Commanders. The Education Classes were held as usual. Battalion Pay Parade.	
...do...	13/1/19		Companies at the disposal of Company Commanders. Major H.G.P.McIlroy, "D" Coy attached to 15th Squadron R.A.F. for course of instruction. The usual classes of instruction were held. A Debate was held in the Cinema Hut at 1000 hrs. Subject, "Is Professionalism Spoiling Sport". For. Lieut. L.Messon and Sgt Telfer. Against, Lt.Lucas & Capt. T.S.Roge son,G.F.attached	

COMMANDING 17 BATTN. M.G. CORPS
LIEUT COLONEL

Army Form C. 2118.

WAR DIARY
or
INTELLIGENCE SUMMARY. Confidential.
(Erase heading not required.)

Instructions regarding War Diaries and Intelligence Summaries are contained in F.S. Regs., Part II. and the Staff Manual respectively. Title pages will be prepared in manuscript.

Place	Date	Hour	Summary of Events and Information	Remarks and references to Appendices
LE QUESNOY SUR AIRAINES	14/1/19.		Companies at the disposal of company commanders. No.1532274.L/Cpl.Skinner, died from gunshot wound.	
...do...	15/1/19		Companies at the disposal of company commanders. Battalion Football Team met the 155 A.F.A.Bde in the Divisional Football Competition. Major.J.S.Gowring, Lieut.F.K.Earle, 2/Lieut.Looms. W.R.D. struck off strength on proceeding to U.K. for demobilisation. 2/Lieut.Haughton,J.R., Lieut.M.W.Penman, Capt.F.H.Arnold, Result of Football Match. 17th Battalion M.G.C....0. 155 R.F.A.Bde....0.	
...do...	16/1/19.		Companies at the disposal of company commanders. Battalion Football team replayed Divisional Compet tion tie, Result, 17th Bn.M.G.C....4...155 R.F.A.Bde.....2.	
...do...	17-1-19.		Companies at the disposal of Company Commanders. Usual parades etc. carried out. Whist Drive held at 17.00 hrs.	
...do...	18-1-19.		Companies at the disposal of Company Commanders. Major Kinsey granted leave to U.K. from 17-1-19 to 31-1-19.	
...do...	19-1-19.		All Companies attended Divine Service at 1000 hrs.	
...do...	20-1-19.		Companies at the disposal of company Commanders. Battalion pay& parade by Companies. "A" &"B". Companies bathed and received clean clothing.	
...do...	21-1-19.		Usual parades and fatigues carried out. "C" & "D" Companies bathed and clean clothing issued. Usual educational classes held.	
...do...	22-1-19.		Companies at the disposal of company commanders. Battalion Played 2nd Round	
...do...	23-1-19.		Companies at the disposal of company commanders. of Divisional Football Competition against 10th Lancs.Fusrs, Result, 17th M.G.C....1. 10th Lancs.Fusrs....Nil.	
...do...	24-1-19.		Usual parades, and inspections carried out. Cross Country run took place at 1400 hrs. Lieut.M.Roberts and 2/Lieut.H.A.Disney struck off strength on departing to U.K. for demobilisation.	
...do...	25-1-19.		Commanding Officer's Inspection of billets. Major.E.M.Thomas rejoined from leave. Whist Drive held at 1700 hrs in the Cinema Hut.	
...do...	26-1-19.		All Companies attended Divine Services at 1130 hrs in the Cinema Hut.	

Army Form C. 2118.

WAR DIARY
or
INTELLIGENCE SUMMARY

Confidential.

(Erase heading not required.)

Instructions regarding War Diaries and Intelligence Summaries are contained in F.S. Regs., Part II and the Staff Manual respectively. Title pages will be prepared in manuscript.

Place	Date	Hour	Summary of Events and Information	Remarks and references to Appendices
LE QUESNOY SUR AIRAINES.	27-1-19.		Usual parades etc. carried out. "A" & "B" Coys bathed and clean clothing issued. Iron rations withdrawn in accordance with G.R.O.. Battalion Football Team played the 3rd round of the Divisional Football Competition, against the 78th Bde.R.F.A. Result. 78th Bde R.F.A....3....17th M.G.C....Nil. Battalion paid.	
...do...	28-1-19.		Companies at the disposal of company commanders. "C" & "D" Coys bathed and clean clothing issued. Lecture by Pte Blyth, Subject, "The Five States of Central America".	
...do...	29-1-19.		Companies at the disposal of company commanders. 2/Lieut.A.C.Wylde appointed Company Transport Officer vice Lieut.R.G.Bond to U.K. for demobilisation. Capt. & Rev. T.B.Rogerson granted leave to U.K. from 21-1-19 to 12-2-19. Lecture by Capt. & Adjt., A.McInnes. Subject, "Capital".	
...do...	30-1-19.		Companies at the disposal of Company Commanders. Usual parades carried out. Lieut. R.G.Bond, "C" Company, Lieut. D.G.Latimer "B" Coy, 2/Lieut.J.W Jones, "A" Coy proceeded to U.K. for demobilisation, and struck off strength accordngly.	
...do...	31-1-19.		Companies at the disposal of company Commanders. Lieut.G.Fraser "D" Coy proceeded to U.K. for demobilisation, and struck off strength accordingly.	

Strength of Battalion at 31-1-19.........Officers........36
                                        Other ranks.....720.

-X-X-X-X-X-X-X-X-X-X-X-X-

(signature)
LIEUT. COLONEL
COMMANDING 17 BATTN. M.G. CORPS

WAR DIARY
or
~~INTELLIGENCE SUMMARY~~

(Erase heading not required.)

Confidential

17th Battalion Machine Gun Corps

February 1919

Strength of Battalion at 1-2-19:-

Officers 36
O.Rs. 730

R.G. Rivaz, Major
Commanding 17 Battn. M.G. Corps

WAR DIARY
INTELLIGENCE SUMMARY

(Erase heading not required.)

Confidential

Place	Date	Hour	Summary of Events and Information	Remarks and references to Appendices
LE QUESNOY SUR AIRAINES	1/2/19.		Commanding Officer inspected billets which Divine Football held in the Recreation Room.	
"	2/2/19.		Boys at disposal of company commander.	
"	3/2/19.		23 Other Ranks despatched on demobilisation. Bath parade by Coy.	
"	4/2/19.		Boys at disposal of company commanders. Divine Fatigues. The Divisional Cinema arrived for a fortnight stay.	
"	5/2/19.		Coys at disposal of Coy Cmdrs.	
"	6/2/19.		6 Officers (mainly Adjt) and 117 OR's received on demob. Lieut L Rand assumed duties of Adjt. v. Capt Hastic command of "C" Coy via Capt Ryde demobilised. L Cmdt took over the Infd a/c.	
"	7/2/19.		Boys at the disposal of company commander. 3 Offrs & 48 OR's proceeded to UK on demob.	
"	8/1/19.		Divine Service. Parade (voluntary) were held in the Cinema Rue.	
"	9/1/19.		52 OR proceeded on demob to Dis Reception Camp MORGEST. Baths were allotted to 2 OS Coy. Major Atkinson rejoins from leave to UK.	
"	10/1/19.		Battalion Baths by Companies.	

F.B. Murray Major
Commanding 17 Battn. M.G. Corps.

WAR DIARY

Instructions regarding War Diaries and Intelligence Summaries are contained in F.S. Regs., Part II. and the Staff Manual respectively. Title pages will be prepared in manuscript.

Army Form C. 2118.

(Erase heading not required.)

R.G. Kennedy Major
COMMANDING 17 BATTN. M.G. CORPS.

CONFIDENTIAL

Place	Date	Hour	Summary of Events and Information	Remarks and references to Appendices
Le Quesnoy Sur Avesnes	11/2/19		Lt. D.A.K. Stephens appld Transport officer of "B" Coy vice 7th O.R. Black to U.K. for demob:- Pte Walton of these by form, and sentenced to 6 months I.H.L.	
"	12/2/19		Companies at the disposal of company commander.	
"	13/2/19		76 O.R. proceeded to U.K. on demob. Lieut A. Kennedy " " " " "	
"	14/2/19		Train parade of O.R. proceeded for return train	
"	15/2/19 16/2/19 17		25 O.R. proceeded " " " " Coys at disposal of company commanders Coys at disposal of company commanders 174 O.R. took also grand leave to U.K. Train parade in nature favourites as for 14th inst.	
"	18/2/19		Lieut G. Bush proceeded to U.K. on leave & Duty. Duties of Adjt & Supplies A/c taken over by Lieut D.G.Ell. Coys at disposal of company commanders.	
"	19/2/19		Lt. Col Emerson proceeded to Lewis Gun school conference on G.H.Q. School LE TO QUET Coys at disposal of company commander.	
"	21/2/19			
"	22/2/19			Batt. Train by Ry.
"	24/2/19		Lt. Col. … at disposal of any commander from G.H.Q. conference.	

WAR DIARY

INTELLIGENCE SUMMARY

Confidential

Place	Date	Hour	Summary of Events and Information	Remarks and references to Appendices
Le Quesnoy and vicinity	25/1/19		Sgt. Aiden & Griffin awarded M.M. in connection with recommendation for Peace Despatch. Lt. Col. Emerson proceeded to U.K. on demob. by special authority & struck off strength according to Maps. R.S. King M.C. has assumed command of battalion.	
"	26/1/19		Day played Bay 7th W.Y. Reg. at Solesmes. Result for me, to Bay one 3.	
"	27/1/19		Coys. at disposal of Company Commanders. Upon Bible Conference on game to act. The 17th Divine Cinema arrived for two days. O.R. struck strength on proceeding for demob. During the week training were received in connection with preparation of all ratings to use returning to civilance. Stores preparatory to proceeding of cadre to U.K.	

Strength of Battn. Offrs 28 O.R.s 279 – Offrs 22 O.R.s 351.

www.ingramcontent.com/pod-product-compliance
Lightning Source LLC
Chambersburg PA
CBHW081432160426
43193CB00013B/2257